The Mystical
Sense of the
Gospels

The Mystical Sense of the Gospels

A Handbook for Contemplatives

James M. Somerville

A Crossroad Book
The Crossroad Publishing Company
New York

1997

The Crossroad Publishing Company
370 Lexington Avenue, New York, NY 10017

Printed in the United States of America

Library of Congress Cataloging-in-Publication Data
Somerville, James M.
    The mystical sense of the Gospels : a handbook for contemplatives
/ James M. Somerville.
        p. cm.
    ISBN 0-8245-1710-5 (pbk.)
    1. Contemplation. 2. Spiritual life – Christianity.
3. Contemplation – Biblical teaching.   I. Title.
BV5091.C7S64 1997
284.3'4 – dc21   97-28873
                                                    CIP

CONTENTS

PREFACE   7

Part One
GENERAL APPROACH TO
THE CONTEMPLATIVE LIFE

1. THE DESIRE FOR CONTEMPLATION   11

2. REACHING FOR TRANSCENDENCE   20

3. THE SECRET OF THE KINGDOM   28

4. FROM DISCOURAGEMENT TO SPIRITUAL JOY   38

5. FAITH AND GOD-REALIZATION   50

6. PRAYER WITHOUT WORDS   59

7. THE ECSTATIC MOMENT   67

8. A GOD WHO HIDES   75

9. THE VOICE OF THE BELOVED   83

Part Two
THE HUMANITY OF JESUS

10. LIKE US, EXCEPT FOR SIN   95

11. THE HUMILITY OF JESUS   103

12. HIS UNDERSTANDING OF THE HUMAN CONDITION   112

13. JESUS AND THE FEMININE   119

14. THE CROSS OF JESUS AND THE MYSTERY OF HIS BEING   130

Part Three
ETERNAL LIFE

15. GOD'S OFFSPRING   145

16. RESURRECTION AND IMMORTALITY   156

17. THE UNITY OF CONTEMPLATIVE EXPERIENCE   168

PREFACE

The material in this book represents a selection, reworking, and re-ordering of a series of articles which first appeared over a period of six years (1991–96) in *The Roll*, the magazine-newsletter of the Schola Contemplationis, a network of reader-associates, most of whom live in the United States, Canada, and Western Europe. They are people who are interested in the practice of daily meditation and are open to both Western and Eastern spiritual insights.

Individual chapters are self-contained and may be used separately for study or contemplative prayer. But they may also be read consecutively, since they are arranged in logical order.

Part One of the study deals with the general aspects of the contemplative life. The first three chapters introduce questions concerned with the nature of meditation, the desire for contemplation, and the stages of spiritual growth. The following three chapters examine problems that arise along the contemplative path, such as discouragement, trials of faith, and difficulties connected with the practice of wordless prayer. The final three chapters discuss the mysterious luminous darkness, the chiaroscuro of the life of prayer, from near ecstasy to those times when God seems to hide but is always present behind our veil of flesh.

The five chapters of Part Two dwell on the humanity of Jesus. Chapter 10 asks what can we know or surmise about the interior life of a man declared to be without sin. The eleventh chapter takes the form of a meditation on the humanity of a self-effacing Jesus, as in the Gospel according to Mark, compared with the Fourth Gospel which speaks for Jesus' higher Self and openly proclaims his divinity. Jesus' understanding of the human condition is taken up in chapter 12, as he deals with the inconstancy and weakness of his male disciples. But he could take consolation from the fact that all the women he encountered during the course of his ministry (chapter 13) proved to be courageous, faithful, and, in a few cases, his teachers. Part Two concludes with a reliving of the self-emptying mystery of the cross as the culmination of Jesus' learning process and his life of service.

The first two chapters of Part Three carry us beyond the cross and death to what the New Testament tells us about resurrection, immortality, and divinization, the three elements of eternal life. A third and final chapter recognizes the universality of the contemplative experience among practitioners of all the great religions of the earth. The endpiece, a passage from the *Svetasvatara Upanishad,* elegantly rendered by Swami Yogeshananda of the Eternal Quest Center of Atlanta, provides a typical example of a central theme found in all mature spiritualities, the omnipresence of the Absolute in the whole of creation, but especially in the human. It is a presence that is understood and honored by contemplatives everywhere, whether they are of the Hindu, Hebrew, or Buddhist traditions, or seeking God within the bosom of Islam.

Several chapters are exploratory and frankly speculative. Some readers may find them unsettling, while they may broaden horizons for others, whether by questioning old assumptions or by casting new light on venerable traditions.

I am sincerely grateful to the many readers of *The Roll* who have asked over the years that the articles which appeared in the magazine be gathered together and published in book form. Their encouragement has been a major factor in bringing this about. My thanks to Michael Leach of Crossroad Publishing Company for overseeing the publication of the work, to my wife, Beatrice Bruteau, for helping me clarify or redesign passages that needed further refinement, and to the friends who gave generously of their time to read the manuscript and offer valuable suggestions that have been incorporated into the text. Among that latter it is a pleasure to include Frederick Franck, Dana Greene, Sue Monk Kidd, Paul Knitter, Victor Kramer, Mary Jo Meadow, and John Shea.

JAMES M. SOMERVILLE
Pfafftown, N.C.

Part One

GENERAL APPROACH TO THE CONTEMPLATIVE LIFE

Chapter 1

THE DESIRE FOR CONTEMPLATION

Before we turn to the Gospels in relation to the mystical life and the contemplative path, a few words are in order about the contemplative state itself. There are no available statistics on the number of people who are contemplatives. Even if one wanted to take a sampling of those who are more or less regular in their attendance at church, what criteria could we establish for determining just who is and who is not a contemplative? Many people have brief contemplative moments when time seems to stand still and they are carried out of themselves by an experience of truth and beauty, but such episodes are of brief duration and they cannot be reproduced at will.

The Contemplative State

True contemplatives are those who live habitually in the presence of God. This awareness accompanies them wherever they go, no matter what they are doing. It is a state enjoyed by devout persons of many different faiths, by Jews, Moslems, Hindus, and Christians. Unlike the vast majority of good people who lead exemplary lives, contemplatives have another dimension to their commitment. For such people an awareness of the divine is present at all times, even in periods of spiritual dryness, even when they may feel that they have been unfaithful to their vocation, even when they are drowsy. "I slept," says the author of the Song of Songs, "but my heart was awake" (Song 5:2).

Amid all the distractions of a busy life with all its demands, in illness and pain, during hours of prayer that provide no apparent spiritual insight or consolation, there is always present deep within the soul a hunger and thirst, an aching desire for union with God. And it can be painful — poignantly painful when one is flooded with consolation, dark and distressing when God seems absent or far away. Contemplation carries all the earmarks of being in love. It is bittersweet. As with all forms of desire, which are a kind of hunger, the experience is like having and not having, a species of fullness that only shows how empty one is and how far one is from the goal. This is what Plato referred to when he spoke of love, Eros, as the child of Poverty and Plenty (see *Symposium* 203a–b).

One can temporarily soften the inner tension of contemplative love by cutting down on the time spent in prayer or by dropping it altogether. Join this to a little self-indulgence and a certain kind of superficial peace may be restored. But not for long. Authentic contemplatives cannot live without God. Like the prodigal son in the parable, they will soon feel the urge to return to a life of service in their Father's house. The welcome sign is always out, and this applies not only to those who have strayed far from decency and truth like the prodigal, but also to those who were called to a life of contemplative love and have abandoned their practice.

How does one enter the contemplative way? Above all, one must desire it. While infused contemplation is a gift, it will not normally be forced on anyone. Preliminary to the desire, some kind of encounter usually stimulates one's interest in a life of total commitment to God. This may take the form of a meeting with a dedicated and inspiring person, or it may result from something seen or read. Then there are those who experience the divine in the beauties of nature or through the study of science.

Will meeting a particular person or a love of nature automatically make one a contemplative? A lot depends on what one means by the term. There is such a thing as "unconscious" contemplation, and it may well be that every good and striving person actually enjoys it at the apex of the soul. It is an implicit kind of realization of an inner fullness that does not break out into explicit consciousness but is active in the night of faith. Such people will not deliberately violate their conscience. They may slip from time to time, but they quickly get back on track. They experience a kind of abiding solicitude to do what is right, not for any possible reward, but just because they are persons of integrity. This "anxiety" or concern to obey their conscience is another way of clinging to the God within, and since it is not an off-and-on kind of thing, their will is rooted in the divine will.

So, while these people of good will may not set aside any particular time for silent prayer or formal meditation, they are faithful to their inner lights. They live by a kind of implicit faith, and while the call to contemplation may be something they have never even heard of, the orientation of their wills is such that they do truly hunger and thirst after a hidden manna. This way is even open to those who have no religious affiliation, to the so-called "unchurched" people of high personal integrity who stand in awe before the mystery of life.

Two Kinds of Contemplation

Jesus was forever stealing away from his mission of preaching and healing to spend the night in prayer, sometimes in the desert, at other times on a remote hill or mountaintop. It can be seriously doubted that he passed these long vigils chattering away to his heavenly Father about the previous day's activities. What is more likely is that he centered himself and withdrew inwardly into a deeper and deeper silence. He needed to plug into the divine source and recharge his spiritual batteries. That he experienced what the mystics call infused contemplation can scarcely be doubted. And it is this kind of contemplation that would seem to be referred to when we read in the Gospels that many are called (to a devout life), but few are chosen for the life of explicit, conscious, infused contemplation.

Whether or not one is chosen for the more unmistakably mystical type of contemplation, the fact remains that those who live by faith are gifted with a more hidden kind of union with God. Heaven is realized on earth for both types of contemplatives because the spirit is anchored through the veil of time to that which is eternal. While the higher form of contemplation is a great gift, it also entails great responsibilities: "To whom much has been given, of that one much will be required" (Luke 12:48). Usually, in secular life as well as in religious, unusual gifts are accorded men and women so that they may be of service to others. In the world to come, those who have enjoyed the more explicit and conscious forms of contemplation may not turn out to be closer to God than those who lived by faith with few spiritual visitations.

The vast majority of stories and admonitions which Jesus proposed can be read on the more obvious moralistic level, and they usually are so understood and preached. But they also have a more hidden, esoteric, inner meaning which has to do with contemplation. When Jesus speaks about hidden treasure, the pearl of great price, or about seeking first the kingdom of heaven, he is not talking about joining a particular Christian church or denomination, but about the contemplative path. When he urges all to "ask" that they may receive and "seek" that they may find, it is not a question of seeking and finding the one true religion, but about contemplative union with God. This is the way that is hidden from the wise and advantaged people of this world and revealed to the little ones, to those who have not complicated their lives by immersing themselves in vain pursuits and pleasures.

Even the most transient contemplative moment cannot be provoked by trying to manipulate the psyche. By taking thought of it, one cannot add a single hour to one's span of life (Matt. 6:27). The reason is because any kind of contemplation, whether of the explicit variety or not, is a gift. We can and should do all in our power to prepare for it, but as St. Augustine wrote many centuries ago, even the desire for a good and salutary desire is a grace. Jesus, speaking as the incarnate voice of Eternal Wisdom, warns those who would seek the gift of contemplation: "Without me you can do nothing" (John 15:5). But having said this much, it is also true that "if you ask anything in my name, I will do it for you" (John 14:14). We are not dealing here primarily with material favors but with spiritual ones. Moving mountains and withering fig trees by faith would be easier than becoming a contemplative without faith and on the basis of one's own merits, or by any kind of dogged determination. Only in total openness and simplicity is the gift conferred.

However, once this is recognized, then every effort must be made to remain faithful to the call. God will not disappoint the true seeker. The spiritual life has its laws just as does the material world. Those who approach God in humility, with desire, and in love will not be turned away. One may suffer various kinds of material, emotional, and mental hardships, but the will of the contemplative is always riveted to the divine will. When Jesus prayed in the Garden of Gethsemane, "not my will but thine be done," he was indicating the role of the human will in bringing it into conformity with the divine. People so often look upon suffering and disappointments as unequivocally evil, and from one angle of perception they are right. But that is not where the life of the spirit unfolds. The contemplative knows this, and that is why he or she entertains no real preference, or at least does not insist on a life of personal comfort. Whether we experience sickness or health, poverty or riches, desolation or spiritual highs, it is not clear that one of the pairs is better for the soul than the other.

"That Your Joy May Be Full" (John 15:11)

At the Last Supper during his final discourse to his apostles, Jesus spoke seven times of his joy and the joy he wished to impart to his followers. This in spite of the fact that he was to undergo a cruel death within a relatively few hours. The surest sign of the true contemplative, whether the contemplation is hidden or overt, is the abiding sense of peace, gratitude, and joy. Death itself, that unmentionable bugbear of a self-indulgent culture, cannot diminish the deeper trust and inner peace that nothing in the world can bring. This does not mean that one is immune from temptations against trust in God's presence and love when one is afflicted with suffering and disappointments. But they, too, constitute part of the purifying process. No matter what happens down below, the sun is always shining in the highest, most delicate regions of the soul, that is, in the interior heaven where the Father dwells as the ground of our very existence.

Seeking first the kingdom of heaven, then, presupposes that one knows the meaning of joy. There is a subtle distinction between joy and happiness. Joy is more interior, more serious and muted. It does not depend on good fortune or good health. When Jesus warned his disciples that in the world they would suffer, he was quick to add, "but take courage; I have conquered the world" (John 16:33). This overcoming the world does not mean abandoning it. That would be to concentrate on only one aspect of the contemplative life. The contemplative is not a dropout, but a person who brings to the world the fruits of contemplation: love, purity of life, humility, self-forgetfulness, peace, patience — everything proposed or implied in the Sermon on the Mount, along with something not specifically mentioned there: a radiant and radiating sense of humor. True spiritual joy, while recognizing the serious side of the quest, does not exclude laughter. The sad saint is not a saint at all, and the morose contemplative has not understood or fully experienced God's love and the reassuring joy it communicates to the sensitive human spirit.

Indications that one is called to the contemplative path will vary from one individual to another. For some, a growing distaste for the artificiality of social demands and the games people play in order to get ahead may set in motion a desire for something more substantial. Or, one may have reached the end of the rope in a life of self-indulgence so that now one recognizes its futility. Then there are those who from early childhood have had a sense of the mystery of existence and feel a kinship with the invisible world. But the common element is the desire for something more abiding than the world of appearances. So, as already indicated, this desire can take the negative form, as when one recognizes the vanity of all human striving, and this very distress provides the stimulus to ask and seek and find. In its positive form, on the other hand, the call to contemplation is more often experienced as an attraction to silence, simplicity, and occasional periods of unbroken solitude.

As for the ascetical side of the contemplative life, one must, of course, be ready to cultivate an orderly regime of self-discipline. This need not include the quaint austerities practiced by the Fathers of the Desert in times gone by. Such follies only serve to call attention to the body and they are not always inspired by the angel of light. God will not be found in any form of contrived violence against oneself. Far more effective is a spirit of relentless vigilance over the interior emotions and motivational drives that accompany pride and self-love.

Finally, the contemplative needs a model. And for the Christian this will almost certainly be Jesus himself. It is not enough to study him and his attitudes from the outside. One must learn to enter into his human consciousness in order to feel and think as he does. It is not enough to look at him. One needs to look through him, even as we lend our eyes, ears, bodily sense, and mind for him to look through. This interpenetration of minds and hearts not only unifies our powers and identifies them with him and his objectives; it purifies our vision of the world. Try to be him as he looks on Peter or a leper or a sinner — or as he looks on you, but with love. He loves you, no matter what you may think of yourself.

The contemplative needs to have this assurance of being loved by God. The Christian past has been far too much filled with images of God as the spy in the sky and as the almighty punisher of human beings, watching our every thought and action and holding our failings against us awaiting the day of judgment. What nonsense! The love of God is not an attribute which God manifests from time to time. It is identified with the divine nature. God *is* love. And it is a creative love which empowers the one who believes in it. It is a love we must learn to share by entering into the heart of Christ. Then one's whole life can become an act of love for God and all creatures, even those we dislike the most. What fuels this kind of love is contemplative prayer which takes its origin in desire. We do not seek what we do not first desire. "As the hart thirsts after the stream of flowing water, so does my heart thirst for thee, O God" (Ps. 42:1). "One thing I have asked of the Lord, that will I seek after; that I may dwell in the house of the Lord all the days of my life, to behold the beauty of the Lord" (Ps. 27:4).

"Come, Lord Jesus" (Rev. 22:20)

These words appear in the next to last verse of the New Testament in the Book of Revelation. For some this may refer to a second coming of Christ at the end of the ages. For others it can refer to the meeting of the faithful soul with Christ at the hour of death. For the contemplative this coming is not something for the distant or even proximate future; it is a coming that can take place any moment, when one is going about one's daily business, but especially during the time of prayer.

One needs to be prepared for this third type of coming. Many of those scripture texts that caution, "watch and pray, for you know not the day nor the hour," belong as much to the hour of prayer as to the hour of death. Recall the parable of the wise and foolish virgins. Those who ran out of oil for their lamps went back to the merchants in the city, that is, to the world, in order to purchase oil. While they were away, the bridegroom came, so that when they returned they found the door to the marriage feast closed (Matt. 25:1–13). One never knows when the Lord will come. That is why regularity in meditative prayer is so necessary. The Lord will not come if we are not there and prepared. Luke offers a similar theme about the importance of readiness: "Blessed are those slaves whom the master finds alert when he comes; truly I tell you, he will fasten his belt and have them sit down to eat, and he will come and serve them" (Luke 12:37–38). This idea that Christ (God) will come and serve his own disciples recurs again in the Fourth Gospel when it is acted out. Thus, at the Last Supper, Jesus girds himself with a towel and begins to wash the feet of Peter and the other disciples. In all these parables, Jesus, as the Christ or Wisdom of God, represents the action of God in the soul.

What is common to many of the parables and examples is that they often have to do with a supper or banquet. Prayer time is meal time, a time when Christ comes to feed and serve us. But we must be ready for his coming. We can go for days and weeks with scarcely a thought of God or with no tangible indication that the Lord is near. We are inclined then to give up waiting and go back to the world, like the foolish virgins who went back to the merchants of oil. But that is precisely what we must not do. Even if one is reduced to reading slowly a scripture text or simply repeating the Lord's Prayer, the important thing is to be there in readiness for the day he comes. Christ is always coming for those who keep vigil in a spirit of love and faith.

Death as Sacrament

Regarding the second sense of the Lord's coming, namely, at the hour of death, this is not an encounter to be feared or shunned. We all die eventually, but the saints have already died many times long before their physical deaths. Socrates said that the philosopher's life is a continual rehearsal for death. By practicing detachment one dies a little each day. Then, when death finally comes, it has no power to take from us anything we are still attached to. This does not mean that one has lost the zest for life. Freedom from attachments liberates us to concentrate our energies intelligently and effectively. We can do this because we are not pulled in many directions by the demands of the passion or the ego.

St. Paul said, "I die daily" (1 Cor. 15:31), and this dying referred not only to the physical dangers his life was exposed to but especially to the kind of self-divestiture that the following of Christ requires. It meant dying to self and all that is implied in selfishness, self-will, and disordered self-gratification. This is the kind of mystical death the contemplative is called to. If it has been achieved before death, then the death of the body becomes a kind of superfluous pro forma acting out in the spatio-temporal world of what has already taken place on the spiritual plane. In the ideal order, physical death should be viewed as something holy, as a sacrament, since it stands as an outward visible sign of an interior process.

We say "in the ideal order," because, as Dylan Thomas wrote, not all "go gentle into that good night" but "rage, rage against the dying light." Those who have concentrated all their psychic energies in the quest for perishable values are not willing to let go, at least at the onset of some terminal illness. But gradually, as Elisabeth Kübler-Ross has told us, most people come to terms with the inevitable. Denial, anger, bargaining, depression, and acceptance are typical stages the incurably ill pass through. Finally, they accept the humiliation of dying, this ultimate mortification, and they begin to look beyond the horizons of earthly life. It is never too late. Still, a lot of precious time may have been lost, time that could have been used in the love and service of God and neighbor.

For the contemplative, time is of the essence. Every day is a gift. Every success or failure a blessing. One does not live by material bread alone, that is, by the nourishment the world esteems. Jesus said, "I have a food to eat you know not of....My food is to do the will of him who sent me" (John 4:32ff.). This other kind of food is the kind the contemplative is familiar with. Having died to the ego-self and its superficial values, one is at last alive in the spirit. The mystical death, however, is a paradoxical one because, hidden in the soul's inmost center, there is an abiding sense of well-being, peace, and joy. Even as one becomes more aware of one's imperfections, this very diminishment magnifies the Lord. The more we die to self, wrote St. Augustine, the more we live to God. It is God in us who must increase as the self decreases (John 3:30). This decrease and death of the self is what is referred to in those rugged Gospel passages where Jesus says, "Whoever tries to save his life will lose it; and whoever loses it will save it" (Luke 17:33). So whether we talk about physical death, whether accepted willingly or in anger, or about the mystical death to an inferior level of life, one has to die in one way or the other. This is not a melancholy doctrine; it is, rather, the promise of transcendence. It is true, as St. Paul says, "While we are in the body we are exiled from the Lord" (2 Cor. 5:6), and this exile is experienced most acutely by those who have enjoyed divine visitations, or "comings" of the Lord. But the purpose of every visitation is to whet one's appetite and increase one's desire for God.

Chapter 2

REACHING FOR TRANSCENDENCE

"Do you know what you're looking for? Do you know what life is showing you?"

Most people can offer particular answers to these questions. They want success in marriage and in business, children they can be proud of. They work to secure the necessities of life: food, clothing, shelter. They want to be respected by others and have a positive self-image.

These are legitimate goals. But they are not, at least they should not be seen as, ultimate. At best they are proximate ends, which is to say that they are only intermediate goods, limited ends ordered to that which is more ultimate. They are normal, healthy values and are, as such, means supporting the human hunger for enduring happiness.

St. Augustine's much quoted saying that the soul is restless until it rests in God points to the same final ending to all human striving. The fact is that human beings are by nature striving beings. We may be content for a time to run in neutral, but few of us are able or willing simply to vegetate. Those who do are most often losers, because to be adequately human means reaching for something more than what we actually have. This is as true of the saints as it is of people whose goals in life are crass and worldly.

Upward Mobility

It is this restlessness that has fueled the evolution of civilization and science from the primitive Stone Age to the Internet Age and the Global Brain. When is enough enough? Each age is tempted to suppose that its achievements spell the upper limits of possibility. Such was the assumption of the Age of Enlightenment, of the Machine Age, of the Atomic Age. Today we are somewhat less inclined to rest on the achievements of our era. We know that there is more to come, provided we don't destroy the planet by overpopulation or by an atomic holocaust.

The other side of this upward mobility is the impermanence of the vaunted values and achievements of each decade. What seemed to be the last word yesterday is outmoded today. This is as true of men's and women's hairstyles as it is of automobile design. The only thing that is permanent is the impermanence of all things. That old pessimist Ecclesiastes said it well: "Vanity of vanities, and all is vanity" (Eccl. 1:2). In such a kaleidoscopic world individuals seem to be as ephemeral as the world around them. From one point of view this is bound to be depressing, but from another, based on faith, impermanence is instructive. The ultimate meaning of life, as contrasted with proximate ends, is not to be found in the shadowland of time. St. Luigi de Gonzaga was fond of asking, "What good is anything that is not eternal?"

Eternity, of course, does not mean endless time, which would be frightfully boring, but consists in a totally different kind of consciousness. It means entering into the joy and glory of God where neither moth consumes nor rust corrodes. We have a share or down payment on that kind of being available now in moments of deep peace and centeredness. When Jesus began to preach, he came declaring that this kind of peace is already available. It is at hand for those publicans, prostitutes, and sinners who, having abandoned their waywardness, are even now realizing in themselves the new manner of being, while the self-assured are excluding themselves (Matt. 21:31).

Living in eternity while still in the body does not mean that one takes no interest in the exhilarating task of "building the earth," as Teilhard de Chardin used to put it, a task which includes improving human standards of living and the overall quality of life around the globe. That too! We are incarnate beings, living a theandric life, working in time with the anchor of our being reaching beyond the veil of the flesh into eternity. "We have this hope, a sure and steadfast anchor of the soul, a hope that enters the inner shrine behind the veil or curtain, where Jesus, a forerunner on our behalf has entered" (Heb. 6:19–20).

The Anchor

"Ad astra" is among the mottos of NASA, the National Aeronautics and Space Administration. It symbolizes our human ambition to "reach for the stars." The spiritual analogue of this is the liturgical cry, "Sursum corda," Lift up your hearts. Lift them up to what is above, to what lies beyond the limitations of embodied existence. Heaven is our true home, not the material firmament but the truly celestial realm, and that realm is not exterior to us but lies within.

As we walk in the body, we are on loan, on a leash. The other end of our tether is anchored in God. Our limited range, represented by the length of our leash, is also our security. Wherever we go, we cannot fall out of the range of divine providence.

> Where can I go from your spirit?
> Or where can I flee from your Presence?
> If I ascend to heaven, you are there;
> If I make my bed in Sheol, you are there.
> If I take the wings of the morning
> and settle at the farthest limits of the sea,
> even there your hand shall lead me,
> and your right hand shall hold me fast.
>
> (Ps. 139:7–10)

We cannot fall into nothingness, for our lives are rooted in the absolute. We are on loan, leased out to an earthly existence for a span of years, hungering and thirsting for our return to God. What Jesus said of himself in John's Gospel is true of all of us. He "had come out from God and was going to God" (John 13:3); or, again, "No one has ascended into heaven except the one who has descended from heaven..." and some ancient manuscripts add, "the one who is in heaven" (John 3:13). Our innermost spirit always sees the face of God (Matt. 18:10). The truth about ourselves is that, know it or not, like it or not, the transcendent realm, "the kingdom of heaven," is within us, not just externally in our midst (Luke 17:21).

Where Jesus lives, "in the bosom of the Father" (John 1:18), is where we will all consciously live, if we "abide in [his] love" (John 15:10). We are there anyhow, even when we fail to realize it. The human species, called "Adam," was created in the image and likeness of God. The image and likeness cannot be eradicated, not even by criminal acts. The reason why we owe respect to each and every man or woman is not because they are externally pleasing to us, but because there is "that of God" even in the lowliest of people. The "Namaste" greeting in India, where one addresses another person with lowered head, with palms clasped together, and with thumbs pointing to the heart, recognizes the ultimate dignity of every human being as a temple housing the divine presence. St. Paul echoes the same truth when he reminds his Corinthian converts: "Do you not know that you are God's temple and God's Spirit dwells in you?" (1 Cor. 3:16).

Solo Dios Basta

How many Christians really meditate on this indwelling of the Holy Spirit and appreciate what it implies? We spend our lives searching for happiness or, at least, satisfaction. But on what level? If we were to gain the whole world and have every need and desire fulfilled and at the same time be unaware of our true interior worth, we should elicit pity. What people strive for when they are only seeking material gain or pleasure is of little worth unless it is imperishable. The miser thinks he has found security in the money he has amassed. The jet-set personality sets great store by the sense of belonging to some kind of elite coterie. People of no great distinction often arrogantly despise the next lowest social class in order to assure themselves of their own status and importance.

But time erodes our fondest hopes and dreams of invulnerability. Here the television is a great teacher. Your favorite cinema star of a few decades ago now appears on the tube with sagging jowls and a double chin. Flashbacks of a sleek and trim Richard Nixon cast into relief the less vibrant version of the same man as he appeared during the months before he died. St. Teresa's bookmark was a reminder of how transitory are all things human:

> Nada te turbe.
> Nada te espante...
> Solo Dios basta.

> Let nothing frighten you.
> Let nothing perplex you.
> Everything passes away.
> God remains the same.
> Patience achieves everything.
> Whoever clings to God will lack nothing.
> God alone is enough.

Basta! God is enough. And that God, says St. Paul, "is not far from each one of us" (Acts 17:27). Here Paul is speaking to the Gentile Greeks in Athens who, as yet, have no knowledge of Christ. Yet, in God they "live and move and have their being" (17:28). And the converse is also true: God lives and moves and dwells in each one of them, saints and sinners alike.

While Christians speak of the indwelling of God in nature and especially in the human, Hindus are more direct. They say that at the ground of your own being, "You are That" (*Tat tvam asi*). Hence the "Namaste" greeting.

As Paul grew older, he recognized as we all do that his "outer nature [was] wasting away" while his "inner nature was being renewed day by day" (2 Cor. 4:16). Those who have been reaching for transcendence for an entire lifetime do not go into decline spiritually when the body parts begin to shrivel and show signs of age. The housing of the spirit may deteriorate, but this cannot affect the immortal self. We are *theotokoi,* God-bearers, carrying the divine within us. So it is quite proper to respect ourselves as divine offspring, both as children of God and as bearers of God.

This is very different from the arrogance of those insecure people who have to puff themselves up because, at bottom, they do not know who they really are. The authentic child of God needs no promotional effect to trumpet his own worth. A royal personage or one "to the manner born" does not have to pretend, but is secure in knowing her true origin and inheritance, no matter what rung she may occupy on the social ladder. Those on the spiritual path sometimes have to be reminded that their roots are in eternity, in God, and that nothing in this world can really hurt or touch that in them which is eternal.

How shortsighted is the behavior of those who seek to build stout security walls around themselves in the form of money, goods, or reputation. For even after they have managed to "have it all," it turns to ashes in the mouth when one has to face the enemy of it all — death. That is, unless like the saints one looks forward to the dissolution of the body in order to be with God. St. Paul said that to be at home in the body is to be away from the Lord (2 Cor. 5:6).

> For we know that if the earthly tent we live in is destroyed, we have a building from God, a house not made with hands, eternal in the heavens. For in this tent we groan, longing to be clothed with our heavenly dwelling. (2 Cor. 5:1–2)

In Colossians, Paul goes on to say that those who truly seek God and reach for transcendence have already died to what is perishable, and that their lives are "hidden with Christ in God" (Col. 3:3). If we are hidden in God, God is also hidden in us, awaiting only to be uncovered, that is, unveiled, when the glory that is in us is revealed. What the scriptures are revealing here is the mystery of our own being, something hidden from the eyes of people trapped in worldliness, and even from some upright and sincere people who are not otherwise given to meditation and contemplative prayer.

It is fortunate that we carry this treasure in fragile vessels; for if the body did not one day self-destruct, we might be imprisoned in it indefinitely, condemned to "live forever" in this "tent." This would be to postpone, *sine die,* our being "clothed with our heavenly dwelling." Life in the body is a bit like camping out; it is not our permanent home.

World-Forsakers?

No, we dare not abandon the "project earth." We must "work the works of him who sent [us] while it is day; night is coming when no one can work" (John 9:4). These lines attributed to Jesus in the Fourth Gospel are applicable to all who seek God. Life in the body is not designed so that we can heap up merit points for a better and higher station in the world to come. It means, rather, being available to do God's work without the need to feel our spiritual pulse every few minutes. We are called upon to image the divine radiance for others. As we advance in years, the months and days that remain dwindle and eventually grind to a halt.

One can easily be tempted to look back with regret at the wasted years as one's physical powers decline. Could I not have made better use of the years given me, striven more, loved more? This kind of lament may serve as a point of departure, but it should yield very soon to an unbounded confidence in God's goodness and loving kindness. Nothing could be more worshipful than such an act of unreserved trust in God's unconditional love.

Whether one's turnaround, or *metanoia,* comes early or late cannot alter the metaphysical structure of the being that we are, as divine offspring, made in God's own image. We are made for glory, for "what no eye has seen, nor ear heard, nor the human heart conceived" (1 Cor. 2:9). In that life no one is shortchanged or envious of others. Each receives according to each one's capacity to receive, but all are full.

To be alive is to be open and subject to all kinds of experience. We often fail to appreciate properly our experiences, especially the less agreeable ones. When the screws are tightened and we are under great pressure, frantic and not knowing where to turn because of pain, tragedy, or the burden of too much work, we want to cry out to heaven for mercy and relief. Where is God in all this agony and anguish?

Some will protest vehemently if it is so much as suggested that adversity is, or can be, purifying. They suppose that events that try our souls are diminishing and demeaning and can serve no good purpose. Between tears and laughter the fullness of life matures. Some may be hardened by adversity. Most are softened by it to become more compassionate and understanding. If one's inner life is anchored in God, what happens at the surface of our incarnate being does not trouble the soul. Matthew's Gospel offers a teaching story that has Jesus sleeping in Peter's boat while the storm rages and the fragile ship is sinking. What the action story is telling us in dramatic form is that no matter how violently the storms of life may rage around us, God is always with us...within us. Rising up from his slumber, Jesus calms the sea and chides his disciples, saying, "Why are you afraid, you of little faith?" (Matt. 18:24). Whether one experiences a vivid sense of God's presence within us or whether God seems to be asleep, we are never alone and abandoned.

Hunger for Experience

Users of drugs, whether in the form of LSD, crack, or alcohol, seek an escape from ordinary consciousness. What consciousness-altering drugs are supposed to do is induce an instant ecstatic experience or, in the case of a depressant like alcohol, a dulling of the senses leading to oblivion and forgetfulness. So great is the craving for these experiences that some will rob and kill in order to secure the money to purchase their chemical nirvana.

But you can't buy eternity. The most exquisite fix lasts only minutes or hours, followed by the morning-after hell that is painful in proportion to the degree of ersatz mysticism induced by the drug. The only relief from an agonizing downer is another dose of one's favorite form of psychic pollution. What the drug addict is craving is the kind of bliss that cannot be lost. But to achieve such an enduring state of transcendent joy is the work of a lifetime of generous self-donation in the service of others, coupled with many hours of quiet, wordless meditation. There is nothing spectacular in this day-to-day fidelity to a regime of self-discipline and charity. But it is the only sure way that can lead to the permanent fusion with the transcendent dimension of reality, a dimension which already exists within us.

One can understand and sympathize with people who live miserable and frightened lives in abject poverty in the nation's ghettos. Whether they take to drugs or gain a measure of independence peddling them, they are seeking freedom from an inhuman form of existence. Their way out may be antisocial and in the long run counterproductive, but what they are secretly seeking is what the human spirit cannot fail to seek: uninterrupted happiness, the Eternal Now.

Mysticism as Nonexperience

One of the great paradoxes of the mystical life is that at its peak it is no longer appropriate to talk about "experience" in the ordinary sense of the word. The author of *The Cloud of Unknowing* concludes that entering the Eternal Now lies beyond "knowing." Knowing entails having in one's consciousness a representation of the object known. It implies separation between the knower and the object known. But in the most intense and interior mystical state, God is not perceived as somebody else, a separate object of knowledge, but somehow identical with the so-called knower. There is no discernible distance or distinction between knower and known. One simply is that which one knows.

This kind of union lies beyond experience. That is why any attempt to report on the "content" of mystical awareness in terms of ordinary human experience, no matter how sublime, is destined to fail. The coinherence of God and the mystic takes the form of a rapture that is better described as an ineffable nonexperience, an "unknowing," or existential one-ing of Source and self.

It would follow then that any attempt to manipulate the psyche in order to squeeze out of it an ineffable transcendent experience is bound to be misleading. Even in ordinary contemplative prayer one has to be careful not to dwell on or put too much stock in spiritual consolations. We have to look away from and beyond such experiences to enter the Cloud of Unknowing and identify with the indwelling transcendent Reality. Therefore, any attempt to reduce God to "the experience of God" is bound to create an idol. The Hindu mystic says to all such experience, "Neti, neti," not that, not that; while the great Spanish Carmelites Teresa and John of the Cross cry out "Nada, nada."

Do not reduce being to knowing. The attempt will succeed only in encapsulating the absolute in the swaddling clothes of the relative and the finite. God is the unbounded ground of all being, not an object or entity in or among a population of other bounded entities.

"Do you know what you're looking for? Do you know what life is showing you?" In the end it is not the subjective experience of God but God's own Self that we crave, an existential at-one-ment, an intransitive union with Pure Act.

Chapter 3

THE SECRET OF THE KINGDOM

Michael Grant says that during the nineteenth century alone at least sixty thousand lives of Jesus were published.[1] These various "Lives" have viewed Jesus from every conceivable angle. Some have held that he never existed and that the Gospels are a pure fabrication, a story told about an imaginary person. The Docetists maintained that the man who appeared to die on the cross was an apparition, since if Jesus was divine he could not really suffer and die. The more credible approaches to the person of Jesus can be ranged under such headings as Higher Criticism, Form Criticism, and the Search for the Historical Jesus, or under the various forms and degrees of conservative exegesis. Finally, there was, and still is, the fairly common belief that the man Jesus who died in Palestine two thousand years ago will come again, very soon, in the clouds to usher in the Great Rapture when the dead will rise and the living "shall be caught up together with them in the clouds to meet the Lord in the air" (1 Thess. 4:16–17). Paul thought that the injunctions of Jesus to "watch and pray" had to do with the Parousia, for "the day of the Lord will come like a thief in the night" (1 Thess. 5:2). As time passed and there was no second coming, Paul appears to have modified his expectation of an imminent end. Others did not. Even today televangelists are still warning their hearers that the end is near and that donations will be gratefully received in order to familiarize the masses with the need to prepare for the Day of Wrath.

Whatever value the various approaches to Jesus may have — and the more scientifically oriented ones can be a help in providing us with an understanding of who Jesus was or thought he was — most of them succeed in missing almost entirely what I would call the "open secret" written all over the Gospel accounts. Without excluding the importance of exterior works of charity, what I am referring to is the call of the Gospels to recognize the primacy of the interior life and the kingdom

---

1. *An Historian's Review of the Gospels* (New York: Charles Scribner's Sons, 1977), 197.

within. After all the moralistic and scientific approaches to the Gospels have been taken into account, what emerges is a mystical document, a kind of map or blueprint for the development of an interior life.

It is true that one can view the teaching of Jesus from an ethical or moral point of view: one should repent of past failures, have faith, keep the commandments. This has to do with behavior. But Jesus wants all his precepts to be interiorized: You have heard it said that one should not kill or injure another, should not commit adultery. But Jesus, no doubt thinking about the ninth and tenth commandments of Moses, which forbid interiorly coveting the neighbor's goods or wife, reenforces the traditional injunctions by declaring that we should not even entertain angry, vengeful, and lustful thoughts and wishes in our hearts (see Exod. 20:17; Matt. 5:21ff.). This interior discipline, so difficult for raw human nature, is the first and essential step to be taken if one is to develop an interior life.

Unfortunately, the vast majority of people spend most of their lives in the natural order. They may be good, patient, and thoughtful of others, but their conduct is directed by moral guidelines that have been traditional in their culture or family life. The norms of proper behavior are set before them and they try to conform to them. But such thoroughly decent people, who would not steal or be unfaithful to their marriage vows, very often have little or no true interior life with God. This is because they have not understood or been taught the secret of the kingdom. Very few sermons dwell on this delicate and esoteric side of the Gospel. To some extent this is understandable since, with a large congregation, the preacher will try to speak to the average person in the pews. So he or she may tailor the sermon to reach those who may be leading a less than edifying life or to encourage those who are conscientiously trying to fulfill the duties of their state in life. Few sermons go much beyond these limited objectives in order to introduce congregations to a more interior and contemplative lifestyle. Consequently, people may belong to the visible church but may still be only at the threshold of the kingdom.

The Kingdom

What then is the kingdom which Jesus preached, declaring that it was at hand? It is neither a place nor an organization nor a church, but a transcendent dimension of being. It stands for a new way of seeing. I was once in a tall building looking out just as the sun rose. But I did not experience the sun as rising. It seemed as though I was on a large rolling ball that was turning forward while the sun was standing still. This is actually the way things are but, like our ancestors, we more commonly imagine the sun rising rather than the earth turning. We accept the appearances even though we know better on a conceptual level. That sudden experience of riding the turning earth provided a new way of seeing and feeling. Similarly, when we develop a mystical consciousness, our entire perception of reality changes. Objectively, things are the same. They have not changed, but we have changed. Before enlightenment the mountains are mountains and the trees are trees. After enlightenment, the mountains are still mountains, etc. What then is enlightenment? It consists in a different and deeper way of seeing. I have known theologians and scripture scholars who are exceedingly learned and have, from all appearances, failed to enter the kingdom. That is, they have not thoroughly interiorized their knowledge so that they penetrate beyond the superficial though highly technical approach to the Gospels. "At that time Jesus said, 'I thank you, Father, Lord of heaven and earth, because you have hidden these things from the wise and the intelligent and have revealed them to infants'" (Matt. 11:25).

Unless a teacher has had some personal experience with contemplative prayer, with the mystical angle of perception, such a person's view of the kingdom is bound to be faulty. For some the search will end with a learned analysis of scripture texts. For others the kingdom will be equated with an organization with duly approved members and clergy, or situated as a place or state to be realized in the great beyond after death. But Jesus announced that the kingdom was already present and available, that it was not a visible thing (Luke 17:20) and that those who would enter it should not sit around waiting for it to happen. They should exert themselves, for only the energetic or forceful people take hold of it and enter in (Matt. 11:12). Though contemplative experience is a gift, it will not usually be accorded those who fail to overcome their addictions to self-indulgence, pettiness, and conformity to the world's standards.

Throughout his teaching career, Jesus spoke in parables. Their obvious, superficial sense is clear to anyone who cares to reflect on them. But they have a deeper, hidden meaning which could easily escape notice, unless one is sensitive to it. There is a very important passage in Matthew's Gospel which explains why Jesus made use of parables. Until beginners in the spiritual journey have made considerable progress in developing an interior life through self-discipline and meditation, they are not yet ready for teachings that apply primarily to those who are more advanced. It is perhaps a harsh saying, but you do not feed delicacies to those who have an appetite only for hash and fast food fare (Matt. 7:6). The time may come when their eyes will be opened and they will understand truths that would have been quite meaningless and even harmful to them at an earlier stage. Thus, when Jesus was asked by his disciples why he spoke in parables, he replied:

> To you it is given to know the secrets of the kingdom of heaven, but to them it has not been given. For to him who has, more will be given, and he will have abundance; but from him who has not, even what he has will be taken away. This is why I speak to them in parables, because seeing they do not see, and hearing they do not hear, nor do they understand.... Blessed are your eyes for they see, and your ears for they hear. (Matt. 13:11–16)

This is one of those passages which at first seems unfair, like the parable about the workers in the vineyard, all of whom were paid the same no matter how long they had labored. It seems to endorse one of those worldly pragmatic principles, such as, "nothing succeeds like success," or "the rich get richer," while the poor and the oppressed lose even the little that they have. Life can be unfair. Jesus knew this. In the world you may have to suffer, because in it the just do not necessarily prosper (John 16:33). If you bet five dollars on a horse race and your horse wins, you may get back a hundred dollars for every one you wagered. If your animal loses, even the fiver you originally had is lost. Such is life. An astute or lucky man might invest a thousand dollars in market futures and reap a hundredfold. Or, if unlucky, he could lose the original investment and much more besides.

But notice that in the above passage from Matthew Jesus says that he speaks in parables. A parable can be understood on various levels. One way to understand it is the way indicated above. Winners take all; losers are out of play. And that is the way the worldly-wise might understand it. But not the intimate disciples of Jesus. For "to you it is given to know the secrets of the kingdom of heaven, but to them it has not been given." The spiritual sense of the parable reminds us that grace builds upon grace. The more faithful one is to the graces given, the greater will be the increase of divine favors in the weeks and months to come. On the other hand, those who live for passing pleasures alone will lose all at the moment of death. "Even what [a person has] will be taken away." The only values we can take beyond death are those that have been thoroughly internalized.

As they are depicted in the New Testament, the Pharisees put a great deal of stress on the externals of religion. Unless practices proceed from the heart, they have no cash value for eternal life. A man might give millions to build a school or hospital, but if he requires that his gift be trumpeted everywhere or that the buildings carry his name, Jesus would say to him, "Friend, you have received your reward." You can't take it with you, is what he is saying. Only the interior virtues of humility, compassion, and generosity that have been built up in the soul can go with it into eternity. The worldly man and woman who have set great store by their possessions or reputation or life of pleasure, will, at death, have to surrender them all and feel far more impoverished than the poor person. Even what the rich person thought he had will be taken away. The spiritual person, on the other hand, will not only keep the various values and virtues stored up, but will receive a hundredfold both in this life and in the world to come (parable of the sower, Matt. 13:23). "For to him who has, more will be given."

Stages in Spiritual Growth

Any attempt to teach the most exalted kind of spiritual doctrine to people who are still addicted to the various forms of self-indulgence, to having their own way at all costs, to anger, hatred, and the like, would be like trying to put new wine in old bottles (Matt. 9:17). The good wine would be lost, since the persons still attached to old habits would be unable to receive it. That is, it would be a waste of time and perhaps damaging to the novices on the spiritual path to talk to them about the unitive way when they have scarcely entered on the purgative way. Jesus reserved his most lofty teaching until the last day he spent with his apostles, because it was only then, after many months of training, that they were able to grasp in some faint way his deeply mystical doctrine. "Ah," cried his disciples, "now you are speaking plainly, not in figures" (John 16:29). Would they have understood the same delicate message of divine love the first day they had met Jesus?

A key word in the Gospels is *metanoia*. This, in its verb form, is often translated in the imperative as "repent!" (*metanoeite*). It represents the first necessary step if one is to enter the kingdom. At this early stage it means that one is to regret one's past failures with a firm purpose of amendment. But, actually, the Greek word used in the Gospels has the literal meaning of changing one's mind, of seeing things differently, altering one's angle of perception. In this latter sense, it applies more properly to what has been called one's "second conversion," a conversion not so much away from a life of sin as a conversion to a mystical or truly supernatural way of seeing and being.

In the ideal order we can speak of two turnabouts or conversions, but in practice both tend to be imprecisely defined, gradual rather than sudden. St. Augustine kept postponing his conversion, even though he was well on the road to it long before he received the grace to abandon his former lifestyle. Some Buddhists speak of enlightenment as a sudden, once-for-all occurrence, while others maintain that there can be many little stirrings before one's final grand *satori*. In other words, neither of the two conversions comes ordinarily like a bolt from the blue. There is usually a build up of perceptions which eventuate in a change of behavior or outlook. If the first *metanoia* is a reformation, the second is a transformation. With the advent of the latter, everything is seen *sub specie aeternitatis* and God is seen in every event and experience.

What brings about either of these two conversions is often something that is unexpected and even quite trivial. In Augustine's case, what moved him to pick up and read St. Paul's Epistle to the Romans was the singsong voice of a child in the neighboring house. The child kept repeating, *Tolle, lege.* Take up, read. The passage he read told him to put off wantonness and debauchery and put on the Lord Jesus Christ (Rom. 13:13).

That was a moral conversion. Not yet mystical, it was nonetheless a necessary step in the direction of a vastly enlarged worldview. With the reformation of manners behind him, Augustine could now look forward to a radical transformation of his spiritual outlook. The moral and mystical conversions should not be confused, even though they sometimes do coincide in the temporal order. There are people who from earliest childhood remain pure, generous, considerate of others. Unlike most of us who, in building up a solid sense of self, also become selfish, arrogant, or intemperate in our behavior, especially in the early teens, the unusually gifted child may never pass through a moral conversion, so that his or her *metanoia* may be somewhat mystical right from the start.

But for most, following the traditional path in their spiritual development, they will begin by entering the Purgative Way. Having rid themselves of all inordinate attachments, they move into the Illuminative Way, in which the service of God brings with it the beginning of wisdom, so that one sees God in all things and is forgetful of self. Finally, those who experience God *in* and *as* their deeper self have arrived at union, or the Unitive Way. In this third case, so very, very rare, the transformed life becomes the transfigured life. So we have the three stages: reformation, transformation, and transfiguration.

It is doubtless the experience of most people who practice meditative prayer that their prayer hour or half hour can be dry with little in the way of consoling illuminations. Then suddenly when they are not at formal prayer at all, but doing something quite mundane, they receive a deeply spiritual insight that seems to come from nowhere and to have no "cause" to which it can be traced. Wolfgang Kopp expresses it well:

> The breakthrough to the divine light always occurs unexpectedly, most often at times outside of meditation. Some may be granted the enlightenment experience quite suddenly and in an unforeseen fashion, shortly before falling asleep. Precisely at the moment when we are relaxed and let go — or, better said, when we ourselves become release — will everything be given to us. It may happen to others while reading the familiar lines of a religious text to which their spiritual eye had been closed before. Often the direct stimulus is just a sound: a bell, a birdsong; or the sight of a leaf falling from a tree, or a flower. It was the sound of a frog jumping into water as he sat by an old pond in the monastery garden that became the stimulus for Zen poet Basho's (17th century) great awakening.[2]

St. Ignatius Loyola in his handbook for retreat givers, *The Spiritual Exercises,* says in an Appendix called "Rules for the Discernment of Spirits":

> It is peculiar to God Our Lord alone to grant consolation to the soul without cause for it, because it belongs to the Creator to go in and out of the soul, to excite motions in it, attracting it entirely to His Divine Majesty. I say, without a cause, that is, without any previous perception or knowledge of any object from which such consolation might come to the soul, by means of its own acts of understanding and will.

On the other hand, should one manage to come to some bright conclusion after carefully reasoning it out, this may or may not indicate a divine visitation. It may have a cause in the natural order, just as the antecedents or premises of a logical conclusion can be said to "cause" that conclusion insofar as it is implicitly contained in the premises. Jesus entered the Upper Room where the apostles were gathered together after the resurrection, "the doors being closed." Like divine grace and mystical insight, he did not enter by the usual doors. So it happens that

---

2. *Free Yourself of Everything: Radical Guidance in the Spirit of Zen and Christian Mysticism* (Boston: Tuttle, 1991), 90–91.

when we are not even thinking about spiritual things, God may enter in, the doors of the senses being closed or focused on something else. It must be added that such visitations rarely come to people who do not practice meditation.

The Evangelists probably intended to encourage prayerful people when they included in the Gospels an account of Jesus' agony in the garden. Face to face with his cruel death, he prays for an hour without any divine consolation. Then, seeking at least the company of his three apostles, he comes three times and finds them asleep — "for sorrow," adds Luke in his usual charitable way when he treats the apostles (Luke 22:45). Bereft of consolation, both human and divine, Jesus pleads with the three sleepers, "Could you not watch with me for one hour? Watch and pray that you may not enter into temptation. The spirit is willing but the flesh is weak" (Matt. 26:41). The Buddha said that most people go through life half asleep. We are like somnambulists, sleep-walkers, being born, growing up, marrying, having children, working, and finally dying with little sense of the wonder of existence.

Silent contemplative prayer is not always an immediately rewarding experience for the emotions, but it does prepare the soul for insights later on. In fact, meditation is the principal instrument available to us in this life for entry into the kingdom, or for having the kingdom enter into explicit consciousness from within — the doors of the senses being closed. The divine presence is always there, in back of our cluttered minds. It is mainly in the silence of the senses and the imagination that it can emerge, as it were, from within and engulf the conscious mind.

The Return of Jesus

It is true that some of Jesus' own apostles, even after the resurrection, still thought that he would return to earth to establish an earthly kingdom. Wrong. His kingdom was "not of this world" (John 18:36), which means that it was to be primarily interior and invisible, that it was not to come with pomp and circumstance (Luke 17:20). Anything like a second coming of the Son of Man is entirely absent from John's Gospel. At the Last Supper Jesus tells his eleven apostles that after his death he will come again, that they will see him and rejoice (John 16:22). This coming is represented by the postresurrection appearances. Either the author of the Fourth Gospel does not know about a celestial, public coming of Jesus in the clouds *or*, knowing about the rumor, he goes out of his way to dismiss it by having the return of Jesus take the form of his appearances to a few chosen witnesses.

Even in the Synoptic Gospels, far from indicating that the kingdom's arrival must wait upon the return of Jesus, the parables about it almost all indicate that the kingdom is already present and only needs to be found. That is the gist of all those similes likening the kingdom to hidden treasure, to a pearl of great price, or to a lost coin which people are urged to seek and find *now* while still in the body. Such images are contrary to the idea that the kingdom will come at some future time when Jesus, as the Son of Man, will appear in the clouds to usher in an everlasting earthly paradise. While an ideal social order might be established one day on a global scale, it would result from, or be the byproduct of, that which is interior to a vast multitude, to a critical mass of people who have first realized the kingdom as present within themselves.

God as the Interior Servant

Jesus speaks of himself as one who has come to serve. Throughout his ministry he clearly served the needs of the poor, the sick, and the oppressed. But as the visible image of God he also served, and still serves, the inner, spiritual needs of those who seek God above all. A servant is one who provides for the needs of those to whom he ministers. The thoughtful, contemplative person has no difficulty in recognizing that God is the servant of all by the very fact of being the author of life and of the material universe put at our disposal. Thus, in providing earth, water, the sky, food, beauty, life, and the capacity for happiness and understanding, God is our servant. We should never forget that everything we have and all that we are is given to us by God.

But the greatest service of all is the gift of our transcendent, eternal destiny, adumbrated in the higher forms of the mystical life on earth. As we meditate on the service of God as creator of the exterior world as well as of our interior life, the divine immanence within intensifies. At times our hearts burn within us as we contemplate the elegance of creation. Like leaven inserted into a mass of dough which continues to work until the whole is leavened, the waxing interior fullness begins to lift up the entire psyche, soul, and spirit until there is nothing left of the old Adam. Only God reigns within, our servant God, the giver of all that we are and all that we have.

The kingdom, then, is not to be confused with anything external, such as an institution; neither is it hidden away in the heavens awaiting our entry only after death. If, by some as yet undiscovered process, one could manage to color-code those in all the churches who truly belong to the kingdom, the resulting pattern would cut across the various Christian denominations and would even include vast multitudes of people who "are not of this [Christian] fold" (John 10:16). It would, no doubt, leave out many who pride themselves on belonging to the one and only true church, and on being Christians in good standing. "Not everyone who says to me, 'Lord, Lord,' shall enter the kingdom of heaven, but he who does the will of my Father who is in heaven" (Matt. 7:21). "Do not presume to say to yourselves," warned John the Baptist, " 'we have Abraham for our Father'; for I tell you God is able from these stones to raise up children to Abraham" (Matt. 3:9).

These are stinging words. They are meant to alert us against the error of confusing church and synagogue with the kingdom. In the first place, the kingdom stands for the divine presence within us. We may search for it everywhere, only to find that it was tabernacled within us from the start. We can be in the kingdom because the kingdom is already within us.

Finally, the kingdom is the community and communion of all those who, putting first things first, seek God above all else. Indeed, those who seek have already found. Or, as Catherine of Siena said, "All the way to heaven is heaven too."

Chapter 4

FROM DISCOURAGEMENT
TO SPIRITUAL JOY

People on the spiritual path, especially contemplatives, need to distinguish between depression, discouragement, and the "Dark Night," whether of the senses or of the soul. Depression is a medical condition which may endure for months or years. Its origin can be traced to organic or functional causes, that is, to neurological or glandular disorders, or to psychological or emotional malfunctioning. The result is a lowering of vitality, listlessness, morbid self-pity, melancholy, and the like. Spiritually motivated people do occasionally experience discouragement, either because they have failed to live up to their ideals or because they do not understand, or have never been instructed in, the laws of the spiritual life. At every stage of the way something has to be given up if something better is to be gained.

But this occasional sense of failure and discouragement is not the same as depression. As indicated earlier, people who are serious in their quest for God do have unwanted appetites and inclinations. We have to battle with them on a daily basis. But as long as we are struggling — sometimes failing — these tendencies may not be obstacles to progress. Often the need to engage in the "Spiritual Combat" is the very thing that hones the spirit and sharpens the awareness of one's need of God's grace. Such tendencies, even when yielded to momentarily, are not marked down in the celestial archives as discredits to be weighed in the balance against our nobler aspirations and deeds.

Among the parables dealing with the kingdom, there is the one about the weeds growing up with the wheat. The householder decides to let them both grow side by side until harvest time. Then he will gather the wheat into his barn and burn the weeds (Matt. 13:24ff.). Preachers and writers often apply this to the church or the body social. In it can be found the just and the wicked. God does not uproot the wicked during their lifetime but judges them only after death when they will be properly punished. I prefer the mystical interpretation of the parable. The wheat and the weeds coexist in each one of us, even in those who seek God above all things. When we are born into the world, we receive the human form ("a body thou has prepared for me," Heb. 10:5). As we grow from infancy to self-assured youth, our original form as it came from God becomes de-formed. We develop all kinds of cravings and addictions, inclinations to power for its own sake, honor, greed, lust, self-will, etc. From these basic tendencies we act out our fears and aggressions in such a way that we injure and offend others and demean ourselves. Thus, to add to what was said in the last chapter, we may abandon our original innocence for a state of temporary or partial deformation. Then begins the effort toward reformation, transformation, and finally transfiguration, or what Eastern Orthodoxy calls glorification — another word for enlightenment.

In spite of lapses, we also have our better moments and nobler aspirations which prompt us to altruistic behavior, to acts of kindness and self-sacrifice. What will be burned to ashes at death (the harvest) are all our evil inclinations. Without calling into judgment the fate of people who are truly wicked, what is outlined below would seem to me to apply to those who do sincerely seek God above all. As for our petty misdeeds, they have no negative cash value, that is, as a debt to be paid in the world to come. They are nonbeing. They enjoy no ontological status. Weighed on the scale of judgment, if we are to use that kind of language, they are simply zero, not a minus quantity.

The moral value of those who truly love God is not a resultant based on how much evil we may have perpetrated over the course of a lifetime (call it a minus 9), to be weighed against the good we have done (call it a plus 12), with the resultant a plus 3. The result is plus 12. This is just a clumsy way of working out a calculus of what is meant by forgiveness and God's mercy. The justification for this is based on what Jesus said about the sinful woman who wet his feet with her tears. "Therefore, I tell you," he said, "her sins, which are many, are forgiven; hence she has shown great love" (Luke 7:47).

For those who love much, their imperfections and occasional faults and failings are burned to dust in the fire of that love and devotion. That is why death, for those who love God, is not a passage to be feared but a gateway to transfiguration and glorification. That is also why those who seek God above all else should not be discouraged by their lapses. Ah, but most of the time we feel far from transfiguration. Who has not had the experience of having made some recognizable progress in the spiritual life only to fall miserably into some humiliating fault, whether it be of impatience, overindulging food or drink, insensitivity to the needs of others, arrogance, idle name-dropping, contentiousness, wanting to have the last word? These are all petty shortcomings that people in the world would hardly notice. But such lapses can loom large in the minds of those who have been trying to lead a life of dedication.

Or, if our conduct, after we have enjoyed some truly moving spiritual experiences, has taken an even more serious turn, so that what was done or said would have been labeled "sin" by almost any standard, we are then apt to undergo a real bout of discouragement. How dare we aspire to a life of holiness? In such a situation, isn't it hypocrisy to go back to prayer, especially contemplative prayer? We *feel* anything but holy. So why pretend? Having botched the situation, we then yield to that subtle form of self-love that resents the humiliation of failure. At this point there is the temptation to bow quietly out of the whole spiritual project and go back to being "normal" like everyone else.

There are several ways of handling this temptation to discouragement. If you fall off your horse during your first riding lesson, the best procedure is to get back on your horse immediately. Otherwise, you may never get up enough courage to ride again. If you fall, go back to prayer right away and thank God for the humiliation; it is a wonderful safeguard against spiritual pride. To use human language, the tears of the penitent are very precious in the eyes of God. Or, as Jesus reminds us in the parable of the prodigal son, when the wayward son returns home, the father in the story asks no questions. He accepts the boy unconditionally. Since this section and the whole book are addressed to all true seekers, that is, to contemplatives who normally have delicate consciences, sometimes even to the point of scrupulosity, we are not talking about "sin" and "repentance" in the pastoral sense of the word. None of us is, or ever will be, ideally perfect. We need to learn to forgive ourselves for being human and not yield to discouragement. Perfection is a receding and shimmering ideal beckoning us to make still greater effort. It functions like one of those mechanical rabbits that greyhounds chase in dog races. It's always one step ahead of the hounds. But it does make them run.

Jesus as Rabbit

Shocking idea? Maybe not. Jesus said, "Follow me," an image which assumes that he is always a few paces ahead of those who follow. He is ahead because of the purity and integrity of his life, a perfection we may never catch up with. Still, like the mechanical rabbit the greyhounds pursue at the races, he does makes us run, not so much in competition but as a lure to help us actualize our own spiritual potential. Sometimes, when in the chase the divine Rabbit disappears, we feel lost. Don't worry. He's right behind you in hot pursuit, metamorphosed into the Hound of Heaven. Recall Francis Thompson's daring imagery:

> I fled Him, down the nights and down the days,
> I fled Him, down the arches of the years;
> I fled Him, down the labyrinthine ways
> Of my own mind; and in the midst of tears
> I hid from Him, and under running laughter.
> Up vistaed hopes I sped;
> And shot, precipitated,
> Adown Titanic glooms of chasmèd fears,
> From those strong Feet that followed, followed after.

Whether we are the pursuer or the pursued, the love of God is before us and behind us, now as Rabbit, now as Hound. There is no escape from that kind of love.

If discouragement can arise because we have been unfaithful to our ideal, it can also take shape when no faults are involved. This is what spiritual teachers understand by the Dark Night. It occurs when we are faithful to our calling as contemplatives but no longer experience the kind of spiritual consolations formerly enjoyed. On the sense level, gone is the emotional accompaniment that once attended prayer. On the conceptual level, we may no longer take pleasure in discursive reasoning. It seems too much like work, and we begin to suspect that we are lazy. At both levels, whether it is a question of sensible consolations or the ability to think beautiful thoughts, it seems as though a former gift has been lost. If the "loss" was not due to infidelity, it almost certainly means that we are being called to a deeper form of contemplation, a much more subtle kind of awareness of God. Only after we have advanced fully to a higher stage does it become clear that the kind of experience we are now conscious of was already operative at a preconscious level, as a hidden manna, in the earlier stage. At the lower levels, or in the case of persons who are not contemplatives, there is no awareness of what these interior graces are like. They might as well not be. A notional knowledge of them is not enough and can even be systematically misleading, since there is the natural tendency to reduce them to something that is better known. We shall speak later of this hiddenness of God. For now, suffice it to say that the profane can have no access to the level of transcendence that is beyond their spiritual capacity.

The Contemplative State

Even for those who have had profound and even frequent spiritual visitations, the divine immanence waxes and wanes. How many times in a lifetime is one likely to enjoy ecstatic or peak experiences? For some, maybe only once. But that can be enough to serve as spiritual viaticum for the rest of the journey. Once burned, one can never be quite the same. Those who are graced with repeated visitations — when desire turns into knowledge and love — may one day enter a state when all this becomes habitual. It is truly a beatific condition which no earthly disappointment, pain, or sorrow can destroy. Which is better, a single moment of rapture, one that is never repeated to the same degree of intensity, or periodic highs? Or, finally, the habitual mystical state where faith and vision are barely distinguishable? Who would not prefer the latter? But beware! As noted earlier, "To whom much has been given, of that one much will be required" (Luke 12:48). As with God's "chosen people," being a "chosen" soul is not a luxury to be enjoyed in isolation from the task to be performed. The favor usually has a Catch 22 provision attached to it. Better read the fine print. "Can you drink of the cup that I drink or be baptized with the baptism with which I am baptized?" (Mark 10:39).

It may be better and safer, depending on the individual, to walk by rugged faith, though it is less appealing. The desire for God, which entails knowledge and love, can be very intense, yet it need not include immobilizing raptures. We all have a mission in life; for some it is a public one, as in the case of Jesus. But for the vast majority, it is private. In the most ordinary and unpretentious circumstances, which may include everything from bankruptcy and the loss of a spouse to winning the state lottery, faith sweetens every loss and tempers every success. It is the hidden manna that fortifies the spirit at a level too deep for words.

Joy in Not Having

There is little danger in a spiritual path which develops along the modest lines familiar to most earnest seekers. It will not give rise to any of the self-conscious kind of piety that puts a premium on the enjoyment of oceanic feelings and sentimental religious emotions. They are often only a sublimated form of sensuality. There is something unbecoming and quite commercial about seeking the consolations of God rather than the

God of consolations. Even the desire for contemplation, outlined in the first chapter, is not quite the same thing as the desire for God. The former may have a self-centered element, if the desire is largely aimed at enjoying interesting psychological states. Drugs can sometimes produce similar results, and they are much quicker. St. Thérèse of Lisieux, whose early childhood was filled with tender religious feelings, ended her life on the cross, having, so to speak, to hang on in pure faith amid physical pain and black interior desolation. Yet, living above and beyond almost any hint of spiritual gratification, she found her consolation was "to be without consolation." But, of course, at a deep, nonempirical level, beyond sense and sentiment, her spirit was basking in glory. She knew this. She loved and knew that she was loved.

Faith, then, is a kind of knowing at a deep level. So when all is said and done, it does not matter very much whether we experience many or few spiritual elevations, or simply live from day to day on faith. As long as faith endures, the Dark Night is just as mystical in the inner workings it accomplishes as the most enviable and consoling realizations. Objectively speaking, the focus of faith is not on the particular, clearly defined incident but on the totality grasped in an all-encompassing but obscure way. The act of faith itself — the believing as contrasted with what is believed — cannot be made the direct object of knowing because, like background illumination, its role is to make visible and intelligible the figures that occupy the foreground of religious consciousness. Faith, for the true seeker, is the very substance of things hoped for, and it provides the convincing evidence for the existence and reality of the invisible world (Heb. 11:1).

There is a close relationship among faith, interior peace, and spiritual joy. To a great extent they are almost indistinguishable. In the Upanishads, God or Brahman is called *Satchitānanda:* Being (*sat*), Consciousness (*chit*), Bliss (*ānanda*). Insofar as the human soul is, in biblical language, the Image of God, it too is *Satchitānanda*. At the deepest level it *is, is conscious*, and lives in *beatitude*. Those who have achieved the habitual contemplative or mystical state live perpetually at the bliss level, even amid all the distractions, hardships, and sorrows of human existence. So too does everyone else, though few achieve explicit awareness at this level. As Zen Buddhists say, Buddha nature is not something we *have*. It is something we *are*.

Every quest for happiness or pleasure, even for forbidden pleasure, is an attempt to find something in the external or psychological order that will enable us to have and to enjoy an inner experience equal to the capacity for true joy that is native to the soul as Image of God.

Unfortunately, people with no contemplative experience confuse having with being. They want to *have* money, *have* excitement, *have* fun, *have* power, fame, possessions, *have* sex. Or they may want to have a mind-blowing spiritual experience.

Undoubtedly, this instinct to have and to get does stimulate creativity and material progress, but it can constitute a definite impediment to spiritual maturity, if we remain attached to these objects and experiences once we have advanced beyond a certain level in the desire for God. The moment we fix our attention on the pleasure that accompanies insight, we have given up being for having. It requires a great measure of tact and discrimination, not to mention courage, to be able to put aside, not only sense images and concepts, but also the accompanying feelings and emotions, whether pleasant or unpleasant, in order to become empty, completely empty.

People just entering the spiritual path may find it hard to understand the importance of this emptying, not to mention the dangers that can go with it. If they attempt to practice this kind of emptying too soon by taking up the practice of extreme forms of self-denial, they can easily release the demons of the unconscious and wind up needing professional help to restore them to emotional balance.

The experienced spiritual director will not be tempted to instruct beginners to put aside warm feelings. To the initiate it would seem like rank ingratitude. But if too much attention is paid to sensible consolations, the self enters in, that self whose instinct is to have and to possess. You cannot *have* beauty. It must be left in its otherness, and then, paradoxically, our awareness of our own being-ness intensifies and with it a hidden joy. In truly ecstatic moments, all the lower emotional and psychological systems that involve the body shut down. Now one simply is. There is no longer a subject before an object, knower and the known. One has moved beyond all the dualisms, even the dualism between time and eternity, between creature and Creator.

Don't ask mystics what they know or how they know. Knowing has collapsed into being to become one with it. They have at last reached the *ānanda* level of the spirit. It is a bit like walking on the water in a dream. Do not look down or inquire how you do it, as Peter did when he found himself attempting to walk on the water (Matt. 14:30). As soon as he "noticed" what he was doing, he began to sink. Do not try to *have* a privileged moment while it is in process. Later you can speculate all you want on how this kind of being-knowing works, but only in retrospect.

Moralism and Mysticism

The French philosopher Henri Bergson said that even people who are not mystics can sometimes dimly grasp what the great contemplatives are attempting to tell us when they try to report on their experiences. Even people with no mystical experience can at times glimpse what they are trying to say. After all, we are all created in the image of God. The plainest Jane, spiritually, can at times resonate with those who have encountered the Burning Bush. So whether one has explicit experience of the bliss level of the soul or not, we do at times have intimations of it. The closest analogy we can find to this state of soul is the kind of rapture that occasionally accompanies a profound esthetic experience of beauty. One can only adore at a distance without seeking to have. Beauty, like the Burning Bush and the ground around it which God called "Holy," is sacred (Exod. 3:5).

Why holy? Because the beautiful object or person awakens in the sensitive soul an awareness of its own transcendence, of its own essential beauty. The bliss and enjoyment interiorly experienced are stimulated by the outer object. But this is only because the human spirit is beauty and bliss. Being a clone of God, it can recognize beauty anywhere as cognate to it. To recognize anything, we must in some sense already be it. Like calls to like and responds to like.

Maybe it cannot be helped, but one of the difficulties of parish life for the contemplative is that the liturgy and scripture passages that are read, not to mention the preaching, put so much stress on the dark side of the moral life and the need for propitiatory acts to appease God's wrath. One can ward off punishment, provided due satisfaction is made, whether by oneself or by another.

The language and concepts here are primitive. They hark back to the days when monarchs had absolute power and had to be "propitiated" if one was to curry favor with them and escape punishment for having given them offense. Granted that because of the limitations of language we do tend to superimpose on our relations with God categories that belong more properly to social or legal systems, still it does not follow that such categories form the best frame of reference for describing the reality of God and the world of the contemplative. Doubtless even those whose whole being focuses on God do suffer occasional lapses. But because the love of God, and not God's vengeance, is the primary concern of their lives, they have long since left far behind any kind of obsession with sin and punishment. "Therefore, let us leave the elementary doctrines of Christ and go on to maturity, not laying again a foundation of repentance from dead works" (Heb. 6:1). Christopher Nugent is right on target when he observes that religious denominations which are predominantly moralistic and stress sin and guilt do not encourage contemplative prayer and mysticism.[3] There are even popular evangelists who teach that contemplative prayer is the work of the devil. This is surely based on a misunderstanding of the kind of prayer Jesus engaged in when he slipped night after night into the hills or out into the desert lost in the prayer of silent adoration.

Contemplatives are bound to feel awkward and out of place when the atmosphere of a church service is servile and threatening. As a matter of fact, it can be seriously doubted whether any of the prayers that seem to feast on sin, guilt, and divine punishment induce anyone to turn over a new leaf. Far better, where stout and hearty sinners are concerned, is a more positive appeal to come up higher and begin to realize one's potential as a child of God. We need encouragement rather than threats and those interminable reminders of our appalling wickedness. The reason for remaining chaste, for example, is not in order to avoid punishment here or hereafter, but because, by habitually yielding to illicit pleasure or any other inordinate attachment, we cloud our spiritual vision and dampen the all-important desire for God.

Perhaps those who have no desire for God have to be led by another path if they are to be aroused from a lack of concern about spiritual things. But even here it is not so much a case of God being offended by reason of that person's waywardness as a case of wasting an opportunity for growth by "losing" time. We can pass into the next world minus the coin of the realm, which is the desire for and the love of God, thus having our capacity for growth all bottled up in a spirit that feeds on husks. The explicit discovery of the inner tension of such a state, when it is fully realized and experienced, must be exceedingly painful. It must feel like hell!

Some people do find it extremely difficult to postpone gratification. Their compulsiveness may be inherited or acquired, but it all reduces to the unrestrained appetite for *having* and for having *now*. It would be superfluous to add that our jittery culture makes a fetish of instant everything (buy now, pay later) and has a horror of having to endure a moment that is not filled with a cascade of fast-breaking images (the TV commercial is typical). It would be tedious to list all the ways in which the spirit is fragmented and pulled this way and that by the appeal of the moment.

---

3. *Mysticism, Death and Dying* (Albany, N.Y.: SUNY University Press, 1994), 3.

Contemplative living is very different. Not only does it not require instant gratification; it even looks on any kind of useless gratification for its own sake as a distraction. In place of this, one cultivates the interior silence which gives rise to the peace that surpasses all understanding (Phil. 4:7), a peace of the kind that the world cannot give (John 14:27). These are familiar sayings, but they take on a new life once the truly liberated person begins to experience what, in Buddhist terminology, is called "the bliss of emptiness or nothingness." Not only is the seeker empty of self but God is experienced as the unbounded formless, as a vast sea of energy in which the contemplative lives and moves, scarcely able to distinguish oneself from the "no-thingness" of God. Bliss indeed, but not as the world gives. In such an encounter there can be no thought of sin and punishment because this is heaven — St. Paul's third heaven — when "he heard things that cannot be told, which man may not utter" (2 Cor. 12:2–4).

In all the religions of the world there are people, lettered as well as unlettered, who are aware of these laws of the spiritual life. They may differ from one another in creed, code, and cult, but the mystical experience of those who seek the Face of God does not differ very much. In the West, the kingdom of heaven is the code word we use to designate this deeper realm of the spirit. Something like it is shared by persons coming out of very different traditions. At the deepest level we all converge, regardless of the different names we use to call upon the Lord. As we read in the Rig Veda, among the earliest of the written scriptures of the world, "Truth is one, the wise call it by different names" (1, 168, 46).

Elitism?

Members of religious cults are, quite regularly, exposed to the temptation to regard themselves as the elect and all those outside the group as little more than spiritual ignoramuses. There are many forms of this kind of Gnosticism, which sets off the people who are in the know from the vulgar *massa damnata*, meaning everybody else. Christian sects and denominations have succumbed to exclusivism, which is now and has always been the form Gnostic elitism takes in the West. This does not represent the preaching of Jesus. What he did preach has more to do with what takes place within a particular religious group than with a negative attitude to outside groups. He was well aware of the fact that his own people were not hearing him. It is as true today as it was in his time that there are people who go through life with all their psychic energies focused on their own good pleasure. Having ears to hear, they do not hear, and having eyes to see, they remain blind.

But Jesus did not dismiss such people out of hand, consigning them to outer darkness. Out of compassion he did warn them, urging them to wake up. His mission was precisely to and for such unpromising people. If, then, throughout this study, I have contrasted people whose horizons are limited to worldly concerns with those who seek God above all else, it is not out of a spirit of snobism of the "we're better than you are" sort. No, people who do follow the contemplative path need to be reassured that they are not unbalanced misfits because they resist secular mores and peer-group pressure. "Do not be conformed to this world," warned St. Paul in writing to the Romans (Rom. 12:2). There is something better, and in 1 Corinthians he offers charity as "a more excellent way" (1 Cor. 12:31). The very purpose of the Gospel is to awaken people to their true nature and vocation and help them realize who they are. This is just the opposite of elitism. Far from wanting to exclude others, it seeks to invite all to share in the riches of eternal life. No doubt, there are missionaries whose misguided zeal is more geared to capturing souls for Christ and their particular denomination — not infrequently at the expense of some other well-established Christian church — than in deepening the prayer life of their own communicants.

Not all of us are equipped by nature to dedicate ourselves to the contemplative form of prayer, but those who do would have missed an essential element in their vocation were they to despise or scorn those who choose a different path to God. None is exempt from the obligation to try to live a blameless life and serve the needs of others by charitable works. While the long tradition of both Eastern and Western Christianity sets great store by the excellence of the contemplative path, it is always in conjunction with the imperative to engage in acts of charity. No one is more concerned about the welfare and well-being of the nations of the world and their populations than the contemplative. Ideally, he or she does not hole up in a cave or perch on a mountaintop contemplating the void. Like Jesus, the greatest of the contemplatives were also the great activists and creative geniuses whose lives were dedicated to helping others share in their own interior riches. It is not elitism when the more advanced and proficient want nothing more than to enable others to enjoy their own blessings. To stir people to begin to take an interest in this more excellent way, it is often necessary to point out to them how shallow and impoverished their lives have been. Jesus did this not because he despised, e.g., the Pharisees, but to invite them to share in a higher form of authenticity. And it is often the case that when a person begins to feel discouraged about the course of his or her life, this is precisely the time when some chance remark of a friend or even an adversary can awaken in the heart a conviction about the need to seek the things that are above.

Chapter 5

FAITH AND GOD-REALIZATION

Faith is not a blind leap in the dark. St. Augustine, treating the act of faith, wrote, "Greatly cherish the intellect" (*Intellectum valde ama*). At the start faith is more like an educated guess, where the evidence is sufficient to convince a person of ordinary intelligence and good will but not enough to compel assent. This leaves room for freedom.

St. Paul writes, with respect to the existence of God, that God's invisible nature is "clearly perceived in the things that are made" (Rom. 1:20). How clearly God's existence is perceived depends to a great extent on a person's openness to the possibility of a transcendent order. An extremely self-enclosed or self-important person, one afflicted with intellectual arrogance, may have developed a psychological obstacle that makes openness difficult. Though they may not be victims of such intellectual barriers, people who are in bondage to dehumanizing addictions which limit their freedom often find it difficult to perceive evidence for the existence of an invisible world. To still others, the existence of physical and moral evil is a block to faith in the existence of a Supreme Being who is supposed to be good and all powerful. The typical objection, dating back to the time of Democritus (fl. circa 400 B.C.E.) runs as follows: If God is omnipotent and fails to prevent human suffering, God is not good. If God cannot eliminate it, God is not all-powerful.

It is assuredly true that if we look on the dark side of human existence, tragedies do exist in the form of disease, insanity, senility, and death — all the evils that so impressed Gautama Buddha. Add to this natural disasters, such as earthquakes and hurricanes which often kill many thousands, and it may appear that if there is anyone in charge of the universe, he, she, or they are either powerless to prevent suffering and death or stony-hearted to an extreme degree. So we are back to the original complaint: If there is a God, that God is either immoral or unable to prevent evil. Or, are we to close our eyes and mumble, "It is not for us to ask the reason why"?

On the other hand, those who are well read and have eyes to see cannot but marvel at the extraordinary complexity of this evolving universe. Out of the original fireball, when matter was distilling out of pure energy, there has developed, at least on one planet — our own — living organisms so marvelously constructed that a person with even a modicum of faith can only stand in awe before the ingenuity nature reveals. Given the fact that we are all made out of chemicals and the dust of third-generation stars, how can we fail to be impressed by the skill of the accomplished concert pianist or the body control of a champion Olympic diver? Yet that splendid organism, capable of such mastery, began as a single fertilized cell whose genetic material, the DNA — a mere clutch of chemicals — programmed the development of the original egg until it became, not a chicken, a tiger, or a petunia, but a member of the human family.

People familiar with genetics can, at times, become too familiar, just as we can become too used to sunrise and the seasons, so that we take them for granted, failing to be astonished by their beauty and regularity or by the fact that anything exists. For example, the DNA ladder, composed of nucleotides, codes in groups of three for amino acids in particular orders to make particular proteins. These in turn are elements in determining not only the species of the organism to be conceived and born but also the very characteristics of that being's constitution and appearance. This is so extraordinary that a truly contemplative person can only worship in silence. It is a great error to suppose that science is opposed to religion. It is, in fact, a most convincing ally.

Aristotle, wise man that he was, placed contemplation as the highest form of human activity. The contemplative lives almost perpetually in a state of awe and wonder. Why should a strand of chemicals lodged in the nucleus of a reproductive cell develop into an infant with tiny fingernails, eyelashes, and unique fingerprints — let alone into a Shakespeare or an Einstein? Why should the difference of a single chromosome in the generative cell produce a female rather than a male with some of the physical, mental, and inherited or acquired emotional differences sex entails? How can hydrogen, oxygen, carbon, and a few other chemicals cluster together to be the carriers of life, a life which, in our species, is gradually mining and mastering the secrets of the universe?

Organic Mind

It has been fashionable among philosophers over the past two centuries to discredit the Argument from Design as proof for the existence of a supreme Designer. There is some justification for this insofar as the

Argument was developed by William Paley in the eighteenth century. Paley's Watchmaker Argument was based on an analogy. If one were to find a complicated mechanism, such as a watch, in a deserted place, would one not have to conclude that it must have had a cause and that the cause must have been an intelligent designer and manufacturer? Similarly, once one recognizes how marvelously complex the material organism is — consider the structure and function of the eye — does this not argue to the existence of God as the Intelligent Designer?

Though not without merit, later thinkers have regarded Paley's argument as overly mechanistic. Since it was proposed before the time of Darwin and modern views on the self-organizing universe, it loses some of its effectiveness. Besides, living organisms are not clocks. Clocks do not adapt themselves to their environment, let alone adapt the environment to their own needs as living organisms do. Even those who accept some form of the Argument from Design reject the anthropomorphic cast Paley gave it. If God does exist and is responsible for creation, God does not act like a human designer who must first conceive a plan and then execute it as something outside the designer. Creation is not a *product* of God's work but is God *working* in the material and vital universe.

As Pierre Teilhard de Chardin put it in his various writings, evolution is continuous creation; it is an ongoing process in which an inner dynamism brings to realization the innate potentialities of nature. Henri Bergson called this inner dynamic drive the *élan vital,* or vital impetus. He was never completely clear in his published writings about whether or not he regarded his *élan* as a completely immanent force or whether it flowed from the divine action. In either case there was something more in nature than matter and energy. The directive impetus was a kind of groping, opportunistic urge which sought always to move onward and upward to better and more complex organisms. In this way it managed not only to overcome the inertia of gross matter but use it to create ever more complicated organisms.

Is this design or not? Evolution does not seem to be a completely haphazard, undirected affair. Maurice Blondel, another French philosopher and a contemporary of Bergson, holds that immanent to all organic processes is what he calls Organic Mind *(La pensée organique).* It is obviously not a reflexive thinking mind but a kind of mute intelligence, like instinct, whose orientation is toward greater complexity in its manipulation of matter. It is as though it were answering the command to "increase and multiply and fill the earth" (Gen. 1:21). What is true of single organisms, which grow and develop according to a program lodged in the genes, is also true on a cosmic scale, as the universe expands and multiplies into galaxies and star systems, some of which have planets and, in our case, life. Time hatches the cosmic egg.

The Evidence for Faith

To return to a favorite passage from Hebrews, faith provides us with "the very substance of things hoped for, and the convincing evidence for the existence of the invisible world" (Heb. 11:1). There are various translations of this passage found in the Greek New Testament. In spite of all the ingenuity exercised by later translators, the King James Version seems to be the best, for it translates *hypostasis* as substance and *elegchos* as evidence. The Revised Standard Version translates this verse as, "Faith is the assurance of things hoped for, the conviction of things not seen." What the translators have done is to turn objective words like "substance" and "evidence" into subjective ones like "assurance" and "conviction." They did this because they want to represent faith as an action or operation of the spirit. Fair enough. But the Greek does not say quite that, and the Latin Vulgate agrees with the King James Version in that it translates *hypostasis* as *substantia* and *elegchos* as *argumentum*.

This latter translation of *elegchos* as *argumentum* is especially interesting. Both the Greek original and the Latin translation of the word reflect the law court. The defense attorney provides an "argument" based on evidence in favor of his client, just as the prosecution argues against the defendant. Each provides "evidence," often circumstantial, to exonerate or convict the one on trial. The judge or jury must then decide whether the evidence and the arguments are convincing or not. So we have translated *elegchos* as "convincing evidence," in this case evidence sufficient, though circumstantial, to convince a reasonable person of good will regarding the existence of things invisible. It is true, of course, that no mere human being has ever seen God (John 1:18). However, there are in the visible world traces, fingerprints, vestiges, evidences sufficient to convince truth seekers of the existence of the unseen God, the invisible ground of being.

Beyond this largely circumstantial evidence, there is also the *hypostasis*, the underlying Reality or Substance of the divine, which is already available to us through the indwelling of God in all things — ourselves included. The fact that we can become convinced of the presence of God in the whole of creation is the basis and ground for the reasonable *hope* that we shall eventually enjoy the unveiled vision of God. While hope has to do with the future, that future is already present and in substance (substantially) available in creation for those who have eyes to see, but especially present in what is deepest and most real in ourselves.

One way of coming to a realization of this truth is to perceive the universe sacramentally. A sacrament is usually defined as a visible sign created by God to reveal an invisible truth. For the Christian seeker, Jesus is the Sacrament of God par excellence. He is above all the personification of God's love. Nature mystics may come to a realization of the power and majesty of God. "For," to expand the quotation from St. Paul with which this chapter began, "what can be known about God is plain to them, because God has shown it to them. Ever since the creation of the world his invisible nature, namely, his eternal power and deity, have been clearly perceived in the things that have been made" (Rom. 1:19–20). What all this reveals is that God is powerful and intelligent, but it remains somewhat impersonal. That is why the Incarnation reveals God, not as a distant yet fearsome monarch, but as a loving and caring person. Jesus, then, is the embodiment of divine love. We need such a concretization. When John's Jesus says, "You believe in God, believe also in me" (John 14:1), he might just as readily have said, "You believe in my love, believe also in God's love." When Evangelicals call on members of their congregations to "accept Jesus as your personal savior," they are in effect saying that God is not an abstraction nor is God's existence the logical conclusion of a syllogism. Spiritual writers also speak of a "personal love of Jesus Christ," by which they presumably mean intimacy. Surely, that is the gist of what Jesus meant when he said to his disciples at the Last Supper, "I will no longer call you servants but I have called you friends, for all that I have heard from my Father I have made known to you" (John 15:15). In other words, Jesus has kept nothing back. "He who has seen me has seen the Father" (John 14:9).

"God Is Love" (1 John 4:16)

What the Gospels tell us is that faith in Christ does not replace but supplements faith based on the revelation of God which the material universe communicates. And the new emphasis is on God's love rather than God's power and might. This does not mean that the Hebrew scriptures did not speak often and eloquently of God's love. But it was the love of a God whose loving kindness (*hesed*) was demonstrated by his mighty works and the favors with which he graced his chosen people. But we, creatures of flesh and blood, find it difficult to relate to an invis-

ible deity and to believe in that Being's unconditional love for each one
of us as individuals — as contrasted with God's favoring a chosen nation. So great is our need for an available image of God that the peoples
of the world down the ages have attempted to concretize God by creating idols and graven images to represent what they thought God was
like. The prophets of the Jewish scriptures railed against such idolatry,
and both Christian and Moslem iconoclasts have sought to do away
with any images which pretended to represent the invisible God.

But suppose the "image" was made flesh and blood and dwelt among
us, and suppose that "in him all the fullness of God was pleased to
dwell" (Col. 1:19)). Basic to the entire Christian story is the conviction
that Jesus is the *Sacramentum Dei,* the visible sign revealing to those
who have faith in his name what God is like. And, as it turns out, God is
one who is willing to share in our pain. In fact, God is now the Beloved,
whose life is so intimately intertwined with ours that our relationship
bears all the characteristics of a marriage. Such is the intimacy which
the contemplative aspires to, since it is the true vocation of a being who
is spirit.

There are, of course, conditions for the realization of this degree of
intimacy and personal love. God, metaphorically speaking, is a jealous
God. What this means is that the full revelation of God's inner life is
available only to those who seek God above all else. Idolatry then becomes devoting all one's energies to the pursuit of something that is
finite, perishable, less than God. When the people of Israel set up and
worshiped alien gods, the prophets called it fornication and adultery.
For the mystic or the contemplative, to set store by anything less than
God falls into the same category. Having been "chosen" for this sublime
vocation, they are to subordinate every other love to this supreme one.
"Blessed are the pure of heart, for they shall see God" (Matt. 5:8). Purity here is not limited to chaste sex. It stands for singleness of purpose
with no quarter given to the roving eye which can so easily yield to the
fascination of vain pursuits.

God-realization, then, means much more than acknowledging the existence of a Creator-God. It is complete only when God becomes for us
a living, interior reality. It is not enough to study scripture and learn
to appreciate and even savor the teaching of Jesus. The work is not
complete until one can declare with St. Paul, "It is no longer I who
live, but Christ who lives in me" (Gal. 2:20). One has to interiorize
the Christ-life that was in Jesus. This is the work of the Holy Spirit
who gradually begins to reveal to those who seek God with all their
mind, heart, and strength that "God is Love." Love then is more than

a divine attribute; it is what God is essentially, substantially. This realization colors every true mystical experience, whether in dreams or in contemplative silence.

Jesus comes to us as the revelation that God is love. Every word and action of his proclaims this truth. And when the revelation is pressed far enough, it will also appear that each one of us, as an image of God, is love. Ours, however, is a love that gets skewed and deformed when we squander it on unworthy actions and objects. But at the source it escapes the distortion it suffers as it wells up through layer upon layer of egocentric energies. At the source, that is, as it comes from the hand of God, our love is, like divine love, uncompromised and uncompromising. At the source, we, too, like God *are* love. Self-realization brings with it God-realization and an awareness of who we are, children of God and participants in the divine nature. The life, teaching, and death of Jesus had as their primary goal the assurance of this truth. The word "gospel" (Old English: god-spel; Greek; *eu-aggelion*) means good news, glad tidings. What better news than the assurance that we are godlings, *divinae consortes naturae*, God's offspring (Acts 17:28), scions of the Most High God and heirs of heaven? More on this in chapter 15.

The Mystery of Evil

Does this revelation and assurance of our divine calling and destiny "solve" the problem, or rather the mystery, of physical and moral evil? Not directly. But, coupled with the revelation of the incarnation of a God who cares enough to share our joys and sorrows, even to "death on a cross," a Christian at least has the consolation of knowing that God is no stranger to the human condition. Were God to remain aloof, watching the sufferings of time-bound creatures safely from afar, we might have cause to complain. But the Incarnation is a kind of divine apology, God's atonement in both senses of the word. God becomes *one* with suffering humanity, and by suffering with us thus "atones" for the way things are. Are you ready to forgive God? What a shocking question for pious ears. Some people feel that God, if there is a God, ought to apologize for the way things are. But this brings up the question of whether things could ever be much different in a finite world with limited resources and one in which the overstimulation of the nervous system necessarily causes pain, while at the same time alerting us to danger. At this juncture God comes in person seeking our understanding for what can't be helped, having in the divine hands the promise of immortality and a share in the divine life. But then the sharing comes full circle: sharing with God once again means sharing in the sufferings of human beings.

Realizing this, the saints have considered it a privilege to share in the sufferings and humiliation of Christ, since this turns out to be the vocation of an incarnate God in relation to creation. The Eleventh Rule found in the Summary of the Constitutions of the Society of Jesus, founded by St. Ignatius Loyola, expresses this approach to suffering and humiliation. The Latin text might be paraphrased as follows: Just as men of the world seek honor and glory as the world teaches them, those who truly love Christ and wish to follow in his footsteps will prefer to suffer calumny, false testimony, pain, and hardship and be regarded as fools in order to imitate and have some share in what was the chosen lot of Jesus. Far more precious are his wounds and rejection than the sum of all the glory and treasure that the world can offer.

This is clearly the language of love and expresses a devotion beyond the comprehension of people immersed in worldly pursuits. If to some it seems quite mad, to the mystics it means entering into and sharing in the redemptive work of Christ, offering one's life and suffering, as he offered his, for the spiritual welfare of humankind. In other words, the redemption goes on, carried forward by those who have inherited the mantle of Christ, as Elisha inherited the mantle of Elijah (2 Kings 2:13–14).

All very well, it can be objected, for those who are bent on a literal following of Christ. But what of the vast majority of people who suffer in silence, like dumb beasts, uncomprehending? St. Paul replies that what they do not clearly realize now will be revealed to them later on. Those who have sought to do the will of God as they understood it have a great surprise in store for them. When the shadows of life fall and our day is done, it will turn out that "the sufferings of this present time are not worthy to be compared with the glory that is to be revealed to us" (Rom. 8:18).

While this teaching is written across the pages of the Gospels and the entire New Testament, it may sound like wishful thinking or pie in the sky to sceptics. It will certainly seem so to those who have no acquaintance with the contemplative dimension of prayer. Mystics and even quite ordinary contemplatives intuitively understand it. Even those who walk entirely by faith have in some corner of their mind a conviction that everything is all right. Such a vivid perception is not an everyday affair, but from time to time, when one is in an especially centered mood, this conviction wells up. It is on such occasions that one understands what Blessed Julian of Norwich meant when she said, "All shall be well and all manner of thing shall be well."[4]

For the man or woman of living faith, the images and metaphors that abound in Psalm 91 are full of meaning. They must be understood, however, in the spiritual sense. Then they assure us that regardless of what may happen to us, to our body, our possessions, our loved ones, nothing can afflict or diminish the true self, the innermost core of our being.

> You will not fear the terror of the night,
> nor the arrow that flies by day,
> nor the pestilence that stalks in darkness,
> nor the destruction that wastes at noonday.
>
> A thousand may fall at your side,
> ten thousand at your right hand;
> but it will not come near you.

To those who live by faith the Lord promises protection and relief:

> Because they cleave to me in love,
> I will deliver them;
> I will protect them,
> because they know my name.
>
> When they call on me, I will answer them;
> I will be with them in trouble,
> I will release them and honor them.

St. Paul, who had reason to complain about the travails and hardships he had to endure, was able to endorse this optimistic view when he said, "We know that everything works for good with those who love God" (Rom. 8:28). And in Luke's Gospel we are presented with the supreme paradox of discipleship. No matter what happens to those who love God, nothing can really injure them, death included: "You will be delivered up.... They will put you to death.... But not a hair of your head will perish!" (Luke 21:16, 18).

---

4. Thirteenth Showing, long text.

Chapter 6

PRAYER WITHOUT WORDS

"We ought to pray always," urges St. Paul. But is this possible? For a lot of people, including those who pray frequently and those who rarely do, prayer is a sometime thing. People pray when they need something, when they are in danger, when they go to church, at bedtime and before meals. And the kind of prayer that is most common is petition. There is nothing wrong with this. Jesus himself in outlining the manner in which we should pray included the petition, "Give us this day our daily bread," followed by another petition having to do with a request for forgiveness for our faults and trespasses. Even the first part of the Lord's Prayer asks that God's kingdom may come.

Besides petition, prayer is traditionally held to include acts of adoration, praise, and thanksgiving. Prayerbooks contain formulas expressing all these attitudes and sentiments. These latter three acts all flow out of the more central and basic notion of love. We love (adore) God for what God is in God's Self. We love (praise) God for what God has done and continues to do in the whole of creation. And out of love we thank God for personal benefits.

Of course, God doesn't need or crave praise. But those who love God cannot help expressing some kind of praise, even if it is only an internal act without words, an act that recognizes the greatness and goodness of God. Adoration is something else. Here, beyond simply recognizing the divine qualities and attributes, we also recognize our creaturehood and dependence, so that we bow down in spirit before the divine majesty. What is implied in thanksgiving is obvious, save that it is not limited to thanking God for special favors or for success. It goes much deeper than that and offers thanks for all that takes place in one's life, whether favorable or contrary to what we may prefer or regard as in our own best interest.

As you may have noticed, there is a twist in the way these three aspects of prayer have been presented. None of them requires words. One can adore, praise, and thank God in a single internal act of love and gratitude. Praise is not limited to uttering laudatory sounds in favor of

God. It is a frame of mind that can be always present. The same is true for adoration and thanksgiving. There should never be a time when we are not partially conscious or semiconscious of God as the center of our life and of all life. This is what is meant by praying always. As I write this the nation's newspapers are carrying a report on the sex habits of American adults. One question asked was: "How often during the day do you think of sex?" For some people, hardly at all. For others, quite often. I wish they had included the question: "How often during the day do you think of God?" For a few, the answer might have been, never. For others, most of the time. Which category do I fit into?

Except in the most general way, we have no need to be petitioning God for favors all the time or even most of the time. Jesus says in the Sermon on the Mount that our Father in heaven knows what things we need, and that we should not be solicitous about what we wear or eat, nor even about where the next meal is coming from. That does not mean that one fails to take the proper precautions to avoid nakedness or starvation for oneself or one's family. But one should not suffer from anxiety. Live one day at a time. Do the best you can and rejoice no matter what the outcome. A similar attitude is taught in the Hindu classic the Bhagavad-Gita, where Arjuna is instructed by Lord Krishna to be detached from the consequences of an action performed in good faith and in accordance with the duties (*dharma*) of one's state of life. Just accept the pleasant and the unpleasant prayerfully and also with good grace — something we can always do as we grow older and wiser.

Prayer and Superstition

During wartime it is often said that "there are no atheists in foxholes." When people are sufficiently frightened and feel helpless, they may fondle their rabbit's foot for good luck or resort to prayer, whichever comes first to mind. But if this is the only time one prays and recognizes a higher power, it can verge on superstition. We can smile at the simpler forms of this resort to religion when the nervous batter at the plate blesses himself between pitches. On the other hand, soldiers will talk about a bullet with one's name on it. This is a kind of fatalism, as if one's demise was somehow predestined so that nothing could be done to prevent it.

I do not think God addresses and aims bullets or arranges for a particular airplane to crash, from which only one of two hundred passengers escapes alive. God is not a puppeteer who causes the metal fatigue that downs a plane, so that 199 heavenly places may be filled earlier than expected. I do not mean to be flippant or irreverent. What I am saying is that the physical laws of the material universe behave in regular and often predictable ways. Accidents happen not, strictly speaking, by chance but because of human error or ignorance. The committee set up to investigate the cause of some tragedy can usually determine what antecedent factors gave rise to the unwanted result. Science does not usually assign God a role in the accident, though insurance companies have the quaint custom of calling a surprise or unexplained event "an act of God."

Persons who narrowly escape death or have a near-death-experience (NDE), if they are brought up short by the occasion, now have an incentive for reevaluating the meaning of existence and deciding what to do with the rest of their lives. Such escapees often undergo profound spiritual and moral changes and dedicate their remaining years to prayer and the service of others.

So, whether we die or stay alive and suffer for righteousness' sake — or for no reason at all beyond the caprice of events — everything depends on the quality of the past life we have lived up to now and how we react to the vagaries of human existence on this small planet. Our spiritual being is fashioned on the anvil of service, suffering, and compassionate love for others. As for the prayer of petition, give God carte blanche and ask not what God can do for you but what you can do to attain a better understanding of the way you can make the best use of the kind of life you now have at your disposal, together with the will to put into practice your best insights.

First Things First

We do well, then, when we petition God for grace and goodness. These first and above all. After that, ask for those material goods and psychological abilities that may be conducive to sanctification. Jesus summed it up succinctly:

> Strive first for the kingdom of God and his righteousness, and all these things [material and spiritual goods that you need for this end] will be given to you as well. (Matt. 6:33)

> What will it profit a man or woman to gain everything the world has to offer and forfeit the most precious gift of all, one's spiritual life and well-being. (Mark 8:36, with a few flourishes added)

Martha, in the well-known story, was preoccupied with the material details of preparing an elaborate dinner to honor Jesus. Actually, from the point of view of one's physical and spiritual health, only one thing is necessary — the one that feeds the soul. Because Martha was so excessively engrossed in food preparation beyond the needs of any of those present, she missed the chance — possibly the chance of a lifetime — to hear Jesus. As far as Jesus was concerned a bowl of lentils or porridge would have sufficed. Mary, who was hungry for spiritual food, had chosen the better "course." No doubt stories of this kind have their origin in something Jesus said or did. They were retained by the evangelist, in this case Luke (10:38), and passed on because they illustrate a spiritual lesson. The point of the story can be easily missed. It is not a question of whether or not Mary should have helped her sister, but whether we do not often miss opportunities for spiritual nourishment while preferring to keep busy about less important things. We need to line up our priorities. True, as the Chinese say, we do have to be concerned about the ten thousand things that have to be tended to in a day's work. Everything in its proper place. But for the contemplative, prayer — especially silent listening prayer — must take precedence over every other concern.

In any case, the Gospels have much to say about prayer. They do not exclude the prayer of petition. "Ask and you shall receive." If we ask properly and with faith, we are told that we can move mountains, or we may say to a tree, "Be uprooted and cast into the sea" (Luke 17:6). Yes, but what is one to ask for first? What is the one thing necessary? Our sanctification and the sanctification of others. This does not exclude praying to get a better job, petitioning that all one's children turn out right, or pleading that Aunt Margaret will live to celebrate her ninetieth birthday.

But what are we trying to do? Change the divine mind and intention? That is the language of folkways. It assumes that God is like a human being, or a being completely separate from us with whom we can make a deal or whom we can persuade to give us what we want. The image supporting such an attitude is of a Being external to ourselves with goals and emotions like ours, instead of being the very root of our life, interior to us and to the whole universe. This is the "heresy" of exaggerated realism.

What then is the alternative? It is to pray with a prayer not directed to someone external to myself, to someone out there, but to that in me which is the cause and source of all that I am. It goes wherever I go because I carry it with me or, better, it carries me with it. We are so immersed in the divine that we cannot see it. And we cannot see it because it is not and cannot be an object. Objects are always finite, particular, and formed. A fish in the ocean cannot see the very water that sustains it. It can only see other fish or seaweed or the ocean bottom. Analogously, God is the one in whom we live and move and have our being. Therefore, God is the invisible, the formless. While it is true that one can be lifted up to an appreciation of God by the contemplation of external beauty, whether in nature or in other persons, this is not the same, as already indicated in earlier chapters, as finding God within. Withdrawing toward the center of our being, we must seek to co-inside (pun intended) with God.

The Mystical Experience of God

In a very real sense it is impossible to "prove" the existence of God. God's existence is not the conclusion of an argument or something we deduce. Most attempts to prove God (to someone else) fall short of the mark and have, in history, produced agnostics and even atheists. For the experienced contemplative, the reality of God is self-evident in the way that one's own existence is self-evident. You cannot "prove" a self-evident first principle. In logic, it is self-evident that you cannot derive something from absolute nothingness, that the part cannot be greater than the whole of which it is a part, that one and the same thing cannot be and not be at the same time and in the same respect, that every true event or novelty must have a cause. You cannot demonstrate the truth of such first principles by an appeal to something better known or more evident, though you can show that to deny them leads to absurdity. These are logical and metaphysical absolutes. In the order of direct personal experience, that is, in the existential order, the existence of God is of a similar nature. Like the experience of a particular hue of blue or pale green, it cannot be communicated to someone else who has not had the experience. The arguments for the existence of God may or may not be convincing to a sceptic. The mystical experience of God leaves no room for doubt because it is, in its own order, self-evident — at least at the time one is having the experience. And it is the kind of experience that has a profound effect on the way one lives. It makes it easy to "pray always."

People experience the reality of God in different ways. Hindus are familiar with the *mārgas,* three of which are said to concern the head, the heart, and the hand. For example, those practicing *jñāna* yoga use the mind to find God at the center of the soul. They have the power to discriminate between the real and the unreal, and this leads to an intellectual intuition of the Self by the self. Those who follow the inclinations of the heart practice *bhakti* yoga, or the way of devotion. Finally, *karma* yoga is the *mārga* by which the devotee finds God in good works and in the service of others, seen as an extension of one's greater self and reminiscent of the Gospel admonition, "Whatever you did to one the least members of my family, you did to me" (Matt. 25:40).

What the three *mārgas* have in common is the fact that they are — or at least can be — a form of prayer, silent prayer, *oraison sans paroles*. The Good Samaritan who helps a neighbor in distress may not be "saying" anything to God, but actions speak louder than words. If he sees God in his neighbor, then he is establishing or reinforcing his relationship with God. That is prayer. It all depends on the motive. The intellectual who seeks God in all his or her studies and reasonings can make this quest a prayer. And, no doubt, the selfless lover, whether the object of love is God directly or in and through one of God's creatures, prays with the heart.

So it is possible to pray always. Still, someone might protest that if all one did all day long was pray, it would not be possible to do anything else. Such a person would probably be thinking of vocal prayer and, most probably, the prayer of petition. But if I am cycling along a road bounded by fields of clover on both sides, where the bees are busy working or a slow-moving herd of cattle is grazing, the scene may bring joy to my heart as I stop and take it all in, fully appreciative of the atmosphere of peace and the wonder of creation. That is wordless prayer. I do not have to say anything or ask for anything.

When you write a consoling letter to a bereaved friend or tip the garbage man or spend an hour or two with a blind, infirm, and senile person in a home for the aged, is this prayer? Yes, if the motive for one's act is to bring peace and joy to one's friend. God has no hands, head, or material heart. Ultimately, it is through us and in us that God acts and loves in the world. This truth is central in all the world's religions, though perhaps too little understood in practice. If, at one time, God created the universe, God continues creating it through you and me. This did not happen by chance; it is the way things are supposed to be, so that we can enter into and be the prolongation of the divine creative action.

For contemplatives, everything is a gift. Breathing is a gift, one I may not fully appreciate until the day I find breathing difficult. Air, water, sky, the solid earth are gifts. The best things in life are free. The next time you consciously take a breath, feel gratitude to God for having endowed you with a pair of lungs through which you exchange carbon dioxide for oxygen. Appreciate the hot shower after a hard day's labor and the cool glass of pure, transparent water so absolutely necessary for life — not to mention for cooking, swimming, boating, skiing, snowflakes, the ice cubes in your glass, and the car wash. Should we not deliberately acquire the habit of looking around so that we may really *see* the riches that have been given to us: the tree that provided the wood incorporated into the house you live in, polished gems adding beauty to human life, the lowly potato or the bean bush feeding us so that we can do God's work?

Even when we cannot avoid being distracted by the ten thousand things, we can rejoice. It is still a wonderful world because God is always at hand, not just in external things, but within each one of us. God goes where I go because, as Paul says, we are temples of God (1 Cor. 3:16; 6:19). Go to church in your local community, but also go to church within yourself, for the divine presence is even more truly alive in you than in any set of buildings made with human hands (Acts 17:24).

For the contemplative, the sweet memory of God-as-present is always hovering at the tip of the soul. This is not a game of make-believe. Where else would God be, who is everywhere in the universe, if not especially within the noblest, so far, of earthbound creatures? People seek happiness — which is another name for God in disguise — in the pleasures of the outer world or of the body, little realizing that God is the "within" of their own selfhood. In the end, after chasing after everything but God, we are fortunate if we come back to the place of our origin.

For us, to be alive is to be caught in the downward-upward flow of God. The human person is the medium for the action of God in the finite world. That, too, is a form of incarnation. Jesus, the paradigmatic Incarnate one, was less an intermediary between God and humankind than an open channel for the divine flow. A window on the Absolute. Can we also be that? Not only can but should. We may not measure up to the full stature of Christ, but in the time and place where we are right now, we are equipped to be or to become an opening for the divine to flow into the world.

The term "Alter Christus" (Other Christ) used to be reserved for those ordained in the ministry. But why limit the divine flow? The faithful are a priesthood for those without faith, and the human race is priest to the rest of the earth's forms, whether living or inert. You are a mystic when you deeply experience this priestly vocation in relation to the whole of creation, when it becomes self-evident that you are God's hand and eyes and ears, God's self-manifestation in the world. Walk around with that realization in your bosom for a few days and you will be walking in a cloud of glory. In such a frame of mind and heart there is nothing, absolutely nothing to fear, neither sickness, nor misfortune, nor death. They may kill you, but not a hair of your head shall fall. St. Paul puts it in terms of the love of God in Christ.

> What shall separate us from the love of Christ? Shall tribulation, or distress, or persecution, or famine, or nakedness, or peril, or sword? ... For I am sure that neither death, nor life, nor angels, nor principalities, nor things present, nor things to come, nor powers, nor height, nor depth, nor anything else in all creation will be able to separate us from the love of God in Christ Jesus. (Rom. 8:35ff.)

Among tribulations, Paul might have gone on to add politicians, the management, in-laws, and the like. But his lyric catalogue of disasters will do. So, we need to thank God in our hearts for all things, for the pleasing as well as the adverse. Can anything separate us from the love of God?

The contemplative, then, already enjoys what St. Paul calls "the first fruits," or down payment on future glory (Rom. 8:23). We see now only in a reflecting glass dimly (1 Cor. 13:12), but that is enough to set one's heart on fire. If it is already so here, what shall it be like hereafter, when the veil of time is removed and we experience unmediated Absolute Goodness and Truth?

Beginners in prayer tend to talk to God or read prayers from a book. This is as it should be, and at no time can we completely dispense with vocal prayer and the prayer of petition. But the deepest kind of prayer is so much more than this. It might be defined as, "The expansion of the mind and heart in intelligent love for the whole of existence, seen as God's self-expression." The social worker prays as she patches up the wounds suffered by poor and frequently ungrateful humans. The biologist or chemist who discovers a new vaccine that will benefit people all over the globe can make the required research a prayer. Even when they are misused, all the discoveries of science help us see into God because the laws of nature reveal the divine wisdom, the craft and the artistry needed to evolve such a world.

Everything can be the basis for prayer. Those who live in this kind of world, where everything simply speaks of God, are the happiest people alive. They, in turn, radiate back to God spoken and unspoken waves of love, adoration, praise, and thanksgiving. It can all be done without words, being simply the overflow of a full heart which gives back to God in devotion what God has given in kind.

Chapter 7

THE ECSTATIC MOMENT

While Jesus was what we would call "an activist," seeking the welfare of the poor and underprivileged and social reform, he was also a mystic. Though the transfiguration may have been the only ecstatic moment in the life of Jesus witnessed by others (according to Matthew only Jesus heard the voice of the Father and saw the Spirit descend in the form of a dove at the time of his baptism), later during the time of his ministry, he spent the nights in the prayer *of* God, that is, in "divine prayer" (*proseuchē tou theou,* Luke 6:12). It was not prayer *to* God or directed *at* God, but the enraptured prayer of union. Neither was it a prayer during the course of which he tried to figure out in advance what he would do on the next day or reflect on what he had done the day before. It was a time spent in communion with the Father. Communion requires no words. As experienced contemplatives know, there comes a time, at least on occasion, when one feels an urge to stop talking to God. Even the chatter of thinking becomes painful. One wants only to be still in the divine darkness, to rest in the Lord.

It is hard to describe this state, say the mystics, but it is characterized by a kind of emptiness, an unknowing, in which one is engulfed in a luminous cloud that pulsates with the divine presence. God is not directly seen but felt as a kind of formless light in which one bathes and breathes. You cannot see the air you breathe because it is both around you and in you. It is your surround, your environment, and your life. The luminous darkness of the mystical night is vaguely analogous to this. If you try to discern forms in it, whether imaginative or conceptual, the state will dissolve and vanish. You cannot *have* it. To try to seize it in order to analyze it is to reduce it to the finite. In this condition, the watchword is, "Don't think!"

Peter, called to come to him by Jesus, who appeared walking on the water, was able to walk safely and not sink as long as he kept his eyes fastened on Jesus. But then he had a distraction. He began to notice the wind and the waves beneath his feet. Immediately, he started to sink. He had allowed his rational mind to kick in, and he knew that what he was doing was naturally impossible. The historicity of this incident aside, the lesson the evangelist wishes to pass on is that we cannot remain enraptured by the presence of God if we begin to ask ourselves how such a state is possible or if we seek to reflect on it. You have simply to be it and not try to put it under a microscope. As Jesus rescues the drowning Peter, he chides him, saying, "O man of little faith, why did you doubt?" (Matt. 14:31).

The words "doubt" and "double" have a common root, indicating twoness. I don't mind repeating that in the mystical moment one must not turn one's attention back on the accompanying affections and mental processes. Simply *be* in the experience. Don't be afraid you'll miss something! By attempting to turn the experience into an object, all will be lost. The moment we try to "get" something out of the mystical moment, the ego-self rears its ugly head. You cannot feed on or be nourished by this transcendent opening and at the same time clutch at its accompanying affective components. You can't have your cake and eat it too.

If Jesus was, as we are assured, a totally selfless person and without sin, his ecstatic moments must have been pure and without a doubling of the mind. For others, too, there comes a time, after the mystical marriage, when it is possible to devote all one's attention, the attention of the lower mind, to the task to be accomplished, while the spirit in its highest reaches is enjoying the kind of continuous union with God that others experience only rarely and in certain privileged moments. Here, the "double mind" is in reality a single mind. Everything is God's doing, an extension of the divine. When Jesus preached, healed, addressed his adversaries, ate at a dinner prepared in his honor, he never lost full contact with his Father. Those who acquire this capacity turn action into contemplation. Doing the accounts or visiting the dentist do not distract one from the delicate memory of God. The soul is always feeding on God. When Jesus offers to feed us with himself as the eucharistic bread, he says, "do this in memory of me," that you may remember me. Habitually to remember God means to be fasting from every trace of self-seeking, not just in one's daily intercourse with other people, but also in prayer. In other words, fasting is not limited to abstaining from food. At times of prayer, one should fast from anxiety, thoughts about money, recognition, business matters; from mulling over old resentments, health, and so on. In order to remember, only one thing is necessary: put aside every other concern and care and recall that even in its most ecstatic moments prayer is above all a form of adoration and self-giving, whose overflow is interior joy.

Morality and Mysticism

Morality in the eyes of some people is tied up with the imposition of rewards and punishments for good or bad conduct. The cash value of good works is often linked to reward, whether here or hereafter. To serve God because it is to our advantage defines a certain kind of morality, but it also describes the limit of one's religious horizons. While a moralizing religion based on law is superior to a way of life without sanctions of any kind, it falls short of a more advanced spirituality.

Beyond the merely moral is the mystical. Here the issue is not gain and loss but a rectitude that is its own justification. One does not attempt to cut a deal with deity or destiny, but lives in the moment. It looks neither to past guilt nor future gain. This is to live in the Now of eternity. It is diametrically opposed to the "now" coveted by the drug culture. What the addicted person seeks is the ecstatic experience without the discipline that is indispensable if one is to enter into the Sabbath rest of the Lord (Heb. 4:5). I said in chapter 2 that it is actually almost impossible to *experience* the experience of God in the mystical cloud of unknowing. This same unquestioning unknowing carries over into one's active life. One responds to the demands of a given situation, not without careful discrimination regarding the best procedure, but without any concern about one's personal convenience or preference. This is not a cold, stern duty for duty's sake, but a loving for Love's sake. True love is grounded in being and not in seeming, regardless of what the other person seems to be. Whether attractive or repulsive, that one is seen as an extension of one's greater self. Whatever I do for the least prepossessing of my sisters and brothers, I do to or for that which is common to all of us (Matt. 25:40).

What is common is the divine center, whether it is called God, the Christ-life, or the Spirit. It is not a private possession to which one retreats, away from responsibility for others. During the nights he spent in the prayer of union, Jesus could not fail to know who he was. But the privilege of having realized his oneness with God and other people was not something he clung to with no concern for the needs of humanity. Each morning, emerging from his union with the Father, he came down from the mountain, entered the city of man, and having thus emptied himself, became the servant-slave of all (Phil. 2:5–7).

He came to prayer not to pleasure himself with the consolations of the mystical life, but to deepen his union with God in order to serve better the children of human beings. But even that "in order to" is too finalistic and calculating, as though prayer were only a means enabling one to serve human needs more effectively. Union with God in prayer is a value in and for itself. Social action is an overflow byproduct of union. The mystic who is cut to the image of Jesus cannot *not* live a life of service. The hermit who has retreated from the world, either in disgust or to seek isolation from responsibility for others, is not an authentic disciple of Christ.

Those two sixteenth-century Spanish mystics, Ignatius Loyola and Teresa of Avila, were both active contemplatives. After his transforming mystical experiences in the cave at Manresa, Ignatius went on to found the Society of Jesus, a work which resulted in his having to become a weary administrator and letter writer, couped up in an office in Rome, all but chained to his desk. But he never ceased to enjoy his intimate union with God. Teresa, great contemplative that she was, spent months of her life on the road founding and visiting her many convents of young nuns, while remaining to the end of her life an ecstatic mystic. So the two vocations of mystic and activist are not mutually exclusive.

Among the lessons that we learn from a careful study of the lives of the saints is that they throw considerable light on the prayer of Jesus. He was able to combine the active and the contemplative life, so that his action was contemplation and contemplation was the supreme action of his soul. We sit at the feet of Jesus when the Gospel is read in church. We learn about his teaching and what he said about fraternal love and the moral life, forgetting, perhaps, that his teaching was autobiographical and flowed out of his mystical experience. When he says "Blessed are the meek, the poor in spirit, the merciful," he can say this because he was meek and humble of heart, poor with the poorest, merciful and forgiving beyond measure. But all this was the inevitable byproduct of his union with God. Citing Deuteronomy (Deut. 6:5; Lev. 19:18), Jesus reaffirms the Hebrew Shema: You must love the Lord with all your heart, mind, and strength, and your neighbor as yourself (Luke 10:27). Not only is the second commandment like the first; it flows from it. And the converse is to some extent true. Even registered agnostics whose entire lives are selflessly dedicated to the service of their neighbors may be hidden mystics in the upper chambers of their spirit without knowing it. But, as already indicated, for the most part many good and law-abiding people are not conscious mystics. The moral life flows easily from the mystical, but the mystical is not an emergent product of the moral. Jesus said to Nicodemus, "You must be born anew from above" (John 3:7); or, "It is the spirit that gives life, the flesh is of no avail" (John 6:63). Just as I cannot add an inch to my stature or an hour to my lifespan by taking thought of it (Matt. 6:27), neither can I provoke a mystical experience by taking drugs or by manipulating the psyche, by sniffing glue, whirling, severe fasting, or holding my breath. The high that may result from such maneuvers has a psychosomatic medical explanation. The peace that surpasses all understanding, which the world cannot give, comes from above.

All or Nothing

While no authentic ecstatic moment can arise by willing it, one can "prepare the way of the Lord" by leveling one's sense of self-importance and filling in the gaps in our response to the needs of others (Luke 3:5). Even so, we will need more than our natural strength to achieve the degree of preparedness that invites the coming of the Lord. Using human language, the old Hebrew prophets warned that Jahweh was a jealous God who brooks no rapine in the holocaust, no part-time dedication, no two-timing infidelity. They branded the nation's dalliance with strange gods fornication, adultery, harlotry (Ezek. 16:23ff.). Writing to his Corinthian converts, Paul admits, "I feel a divine jealousy for you, for I betrothed you to Christ to present you as a pure bride to her one husband" (2 Cor. 11:2). The model of fidelity in the human marriage relation applies especially to the mystical life. Jesus expresses this requirement of absolute fidelity in a variety of ways: "You cannot serve God and mammon" (Luke 16:13). "He who is not with me is against me and he who does not gather with me scatters" (Luke 11:23). "No one who puts his hand to the plow and looks back is fit for the kingdom of God" (Luke 9:62).

Politics is the art of compromise. Plea bargaining is allowed in the law court, but there is no such thing as a politics of the spiritual life. Those who are serious about following Christ must be ready to surrender all. The committed aspirant's failure to do so may result in his having nothing. Understand, please, that we are talking here about the mystical life, not about the ordinary life of keeping the commandments. The true contemplative must learn to exercise dominion over all the interior movements and impulses. There can be no dalliance with idle thoughts. One may give no quarter to resentments, grudges, self-pity, melancholy, one's personal reputation, or even one's health. A prudent concern for our physical, emotional, and mental health is by no means excluded, but such anxieties should not be brought into the inner sanctum when we seek communion with God. "Your heavenly Father knows that you have need of all these things" (Matt. 6:32). There is a time and place when asking for them is appropriate, but not when one seeks to enter into "the prayer of God" (Luke 6:12). This is the esoteric meaning of leaving everything to follow Jesus, in order to be where he is. Where he is, is where God is — within. Therefore, let us "lay aside every weight, and sin which clings so closely, and let us run with perseverance the race set before us, looking on Jesus the pioneer and perfecter of our faith" (Heb. 12:1–2).

The Enigma of Job

It is often supposed, on the basis of ordinary human wisdom, that those who, like Jesus, had achieved the highest degree of holiness and union with God would be immune from suffering and merit God's protection in all their activities. That would be the kind of wisdom that made the fate of Job such an enigma. Why do bad things happen to good people? In a moralistic culture the good ought to be rewarded and the evildoer punished. But it rarely works out that way. Since Jesus was a paradigm of goodness and the love of God, a lover of humanity and a mystic, his untimely and cruel end was not only unmerited but it seems to cast a shadow over the belief that the Almighty is a caring God. That is one possible conclusion that a secular wisdom might draw.

On the other hand, the suffering and death of Jesus might be God's way of informing us that the moralistic view of the divine economy is erroneous. In human existence there is no intrinsic connection between a virtuous life and immunity from suffering. That is a fact that does not have to be proved; it is perfectly evident. And to link good fortune with virtue involves a category mistake. Rewards and punishments have their place in ordinary human affairs, both social and political, but the mystical life situates the contemplative beyond the realm of opposites where pleasure and pain determine value, beyond the locus of the tree of the knowledge of good and evil. The Garden of Paradise, a garden enclosed, is not, nor was it ever meant to be, simply a place on the face of the earth. It is deep within us and is, in fact, what Jesus meant by the kingdom of heaven. It always was and always will be a region in the human spirit as long as a single embodied member of our species remains. Access to it is guarded by an angel with a flaming sword, and only they who have died can return to it. "Whoever saves his life will lose it, and whoever loses his life for my name's sake will find it" (Matt. 16:25: Gen. 3:24).

This means that one must be willing to sacrifice the lower form of life for the higher, the will of the flesh for the will of the spirit. Speaking for himself as well as to his sleeping disciples at the time of his agonizing decision in the Garden of Gethsemane, Jesus sighed, "The spirit is willing but the flesh is weak" (Matt. 26:41). He experienced his own fear and weakness — the prospect of being scourged and crucified on the morrow was a harrowing one — but interiorly, in the spirit, he had never left the Garden of Paradise. The two gardens, the Garden of Delight and the Garden of Sorrow, coexist in us, as they did in Jesus, as long as we are in the flesh.

In John's Gospel, Jesus speaks of his death on the cross as being "lifted up" (John 3:14; 8:28; 12:32). Those who look on the crucified one will be healed, will recognize his divinity, and by this sign he will draw all people to himself. Before being lifted up on the cross, Jesus spoke of his joy at the Last Supper. It was a joy he wished to communicate to others so that their joy might be full (John 15:11; 16:22; 17:13). What the Fourth Gospel seeks to reveal to us in this passage is the continuing ecstasy of joy Jesus experiences in the Paradise of his spirit, in spite of his suffering, betrayal, and human disappointment. In the world he might be the Man of Sorrows, of which Job was a type, but at a higher level, his soul was bathed in glory. The greater his suffering, so much the more intense was his union with the Father. His being "lifted up" was not just an external sign; it described the supreme ecstatic moment of his life. That is why, in dying, he could declare in triumph, *Tetelestai!* The work is done, complete, achieved, consummated. "Now Father, glorify thy Son...glorify thou me with thy own presence with the glory which I had with thee before the world was made" (John 17:1, 5).

At the level on which the world judges, Jesus' death was a miscarriage not only of secular justice but of divine justice. The good should not have to suffer! To which Jesus would reply, "Why not?" At the level of the spirit, his suffering and death in response to the divine leading were the moment of his exaltation. The real challenge to our complacency comes when we are under pressure and in agony. It is easy to profess the love of God when things go well. But when they turn sour, one's only recourse is to the kind of faith that moves mountains. Then, suddenly, the veil of your inner sanctuary will be rent, and you will enter into the joy of the Lord (Matt. 27:51; 25:21) in the full knowledge that your true being lies beyond the shores of time, that "no one will be able to take your joy from you" (John 16:22). Then the flaming sword of the angel who guards the way to the Tree of Life will cease to be a barrier and become a beacon welcoming the pilgrim home.

The exaltation of Jesus in death, his being "lifted up," both physically and spiritually, is an answer to the enigma of Job's afflictions. The good person is not immune from misfortune, whether it be boils, bereavement, or bankruptcy. What the passion of Jesus should reveal to us, and to the contemplative in particular, is that God's favor is not related to good or bad fortune. Nothing in life can separate the authentic mystic from the love of God, "neither death, nor life, nor angels, nor principalities, nor things present, nor things to come, nor powers, nor height, nor depth, nor anything else in all creation" (Rom. 8:38).

Love transcends by far the world of opposites, of pleasure and pain, of good and evil, and the whole world of hedonistic morality. The agony does not exclude the ecstasy. They can coexist in one and the same person. The Man of Sorrows, the Suffering Servant of Isaiah's Fourth Servant Song, is also the King of Glory. The death of Christ is warranty that this is indeed the case. It is not so much a paradox as the coincidence of opposites.

Chapter 8

A GOD WHO HIDES

One of my earliest memories is the occasion when, around the age of five or so, two other youngsters and I "saw God." What happened was that a jagged streak of lightning illumining the western sky as a thunderstorm approached seemed to us to flash forth the profile of the Jesus we had seen in picture books. Since Jesus was God, seeing an image of him was seeing God.

The Fourth Gospel disagrees. "No one has ever seen God," writes John. There are various kinds of seeing and knowing, for example, with the sense organs such as the eyes, by means of concepts as a mental approximation, and by understanding with the heart. The child's image of God is bound to be a very material one: God is like a man only bigger. Philosophers seek to capture God in conceptual language, while the mystic experiences the divine presence in the soul as well as in the things of nature. Though the spiritual life is essentially a seeking, a quest for God, God often plays hide and seek with his children.

In the Canticle, or Song, of Solomon, God is portrayed as the soul's Beloved, who turns out to be an elusive suitor. One catches a momentary glimpse of him, then he is gone. "Look, there he stands behind the wall, gazing in at the windows, looking through the lattices" (Song 2:9). Now you see him, now you don't. His face is veiled and the lattice-work of the veranda half reveals and half conceals him. This describes the experience of the contemplative who lives only to know and love God ever more and more fully. Peak experiences come and go, and after an especially profound realization followed by a period of aridity, one is tempted to cry out as Jesus did on the cross, "My God, my God, why have you forsaken me?" Thus, the bride in the Canticle laments, "I sought him whom my soul loves, but found him not; I called him but he gave no answer" (Song 3:1). Anyone familiar with the laws of contemplative prayer knows that the emotional highs of the beginner are followed by periods of dryness and even a sense of desolation. Yet, each time one experiences the joy of a spiritual visitation, it seems that it will last forever, that one has finally arrived at stability and a true spiritual marriage rather than a courtship. But the elevated state gradually fades and one is back at the old stand, where faith must carry one along until the time of another visitation.

Is God a Tease?

After leading one on, why does God hide, even from those who love him? To use human language, it is to fuel desire and increase the soul's longing; for a weak desire can only expect a weak fulfillment. One must dare to hunger and thirst after God; one must desire without measure. But the pangs of a longing, languishing love can be very severe and painful, as human lovers know when they are separated from the beloved or spurned by him or her. St. John of the Cross in his *Spiritual Canticle* calls this longing love, once set in motion, a wound: "Where have You hidden, Beloved, and left me lamenting? You fled like the stag after wounding me; I went out calling You, and You were gone" (v. 1). Paul says, "While we are at home in the body we are away from the Lord" (2 Cor. 5:6). For the contemplative suffering from the Dark Night of the Spirit, life often seems like a form of exile from one's true home. Once we have glimpsed the glory of the Lord, ordinary pleasures lose their attraction. And as long as we are in the body, even our most exalted realizations are at best only intimations of the capacity of the human spirit for transforming joy. "For now we see in a mirror dimly, but then we shall see face to face" (1 Cor. 13:12).

Throughout the Old Testament and on into the New, we find there is a double aspect to the divine courtship. As indicated earlier, human love is a mixture of plenty and penury, of presence and absence, of riches and poverty. No degree of prosperity, whether material or spiritual, can eradicate the soul's need for more. The Samaritan woman who spoke with Jesus at Jacob's well asked him to give her his kind of water, "so that I may never be thirsty or have to keep coming here to draw water" (John 4:15). In this life we have to keep coming back to the well of human or divine satisfactions since our desires are never completely fulfilled. Having sated ourselves, we are soon hungry and thirsty again. *Qui bibunt adhuc sitiunt* (Those who partake of these waters will still thirst). This is true of all the appetites, whether for food, drink, or sex. Hardly has one eaten than the pangs of hunger set in again. What Jesus promises the Samaritan woman and the rest of humanity is the kind of nourishment that eliminates the need for transient satisfaction. It is the gift of eternal life.

Whether it is called water or "hidden manna" (Rev. 2:17), the trouble with this spiritual nourishment is that it is not palpable. Like radio waves that fill the room but cannot be felt, seen, or heard, the divine life is by nature so subtle and refined that, even when we carry it about within us, we still cannot by taking thought of it easily tune it in. Only after an extended period of purification of the senses, the intellect, and the will can one begin to hear the voice of the Beloved. Several verses from the eucharistic hymn composed by St. Thomas Aquinas stress the hiddenness of Christ in the Holy Sacrament. Thus, in the *Adoro Te*, we read:

> *In cruce latebat sola Deitas,*
> *At hic latet simul et humanitas.*
>
> . . . .
>
> *Jesu, quem velatum nunc aspicio,*
> *Oro fiat illud quod tam sitio,*
> *Ut te revelata cernens facie*
> *Visu sim beatus tuae gloriae.*

It was the divinity of Christ that was hidden when he died on the cross, but in the eucharistic bread and wine even his humanity is concealed. The poet then prays that Jesus, whose countenance he can only behold now in a veiled way, may bring to realization what he so greatly desires and thirsts for, the unveiled face-to-face beatifying revelation of the glory of God.

Quite apart from any theological speculation about the nature of the divine presence in the Eucharist, the material elements, which in some mysterious way reveal and half conceal the Godhead, may also symbolize the divine presence in the universe as a whole, including God's presence in us. "Heaven is my throne, and the earth my footstool," writes Isaiah of the Lord (66:1). The image is still that of a somewhat external God. It is still not a eucharistic presence, with God perfectly immanent to all that is. Rather than the absence of God, the contemplative finds the divine presence everywhere. That is the precise point made in the contemplative's favorite Psalm 139, the one already cited in chapter 2: "Where can I go from your spirit? Or where can I flee from your Presence?" (Ps. 139:7).

Hiding from God

After the Fall, Adam and Eve were said to "hide from the presence of the Lord God among the trees of the Garden" (Gen. 3:8), and Cain, after he had murdered his brother Abel, said to the Lord that he knew that part of his punishment was to be "hidden from your face" (Gen. 4:14). Evil flees from the light instinctively. And this shows us the other side of the coin. If God seems to hide from us, it is because we hide from God. The omnipresence of God, described in Psalm 139, is a hidden presence, *latens Deitas;* it is chaste, humble, and unobtrusive. God will not force the divine presence on anyone. The soul must prepare itself and come out of hiding. It hides by covering itself with honor, self-importance, and material possessions, by burying itself in idle pleasures, seeking God everywhere save where it secretly knows it will find him. Getting rid of the covers and blinders that conceal the soul from itself and from God is the first step. If we may be excused for attributing to God humanlike desires, it might be said that God "wants" to reveal the divine self to creatures. So it is not the case that God hides from us; it is we who hide from God. The divine wind is always blowing; it is for us to set our sails to catch the breeze. Grace is not a gift God gives or withholds at will, since God does not change. It is we who have to change by availing ourselves of the divine resources that are always available. "Ask and you shall receive." The receiving is a certainty, but the asking must be accompanied by honest effort.

Quite apart from human effort and initiative, the vicissitudes and uncertainties of everyday life may compel one to take stock and think seriously about eternal things. In this way the most unwelcome reverses can activate a disguised desire for God. The victim of adversity rarely recognizes the true nature of this desire, at least not at the start. We are programmed to seek happiness instinctively. Only gradually does it dawn on us that no finite, perishable goods can adequately satisfy the soul's longing for true and lasting joy. On the other hand, the rich and successful are not ordinarily stimulated to desire anything beyond their economic and emotional prosperity. They think they have everything they will ever need or want. On the level of what Jesus calls "the world," they may seem fulfilled, at least as far as external appearances are concerned. Who needs God when life is already so friendly? This explains why Jesus warned about how hard it is for the rich to enter the kingdom of heaven, and why he also said, "Blessed are you who are poor, for yours is the kingdom of heaven" (Luke 6:20). There are various kinds of poverty, not all of them connected with material wealth. A mentally retarded man, an emotionally disturbed youth, the lame, and the blind are all poor. Poor, too, are the battered wife and the abused child, no matter how much luxury surrounds them. Such victims of circumstance or human malice are rarely tempted to set themselves above others. For the most part, they have a low opinion of themselves, and because they are powerless, they may be drawn more than others to seek refuge in God beyond the hardship of their lives. Jesus often adds, after mention of his mission to heal the sick, that he has come "to bring good news to the poor" (Luke 4:18; 7:22). The good news he brings to the poor is that God is their portion forever (Ps. 119:57).

Turning Adversity to Profit

There is nothing in the teaching of Jesus to suggest that there is any kind of obligation incumbent on all to embrace voluntarily any of the forms of poverty mentioned above. What one can deduce on the basis of what he says is that personal hardships, regardless of their nature and origin, can often turn out to be blessings in disguise; that is, if they encourage an individual to turn to God, when all earthly satisfactions disappoint or are lacking. Some choose a life of poverty voluntarily. This may be in order to follow more closely in the footsteps of Jesus, or to identify more closely with the poor and the powerless, or in the conviction, based on faith, that access to God is more available to those who have divested themselves of objects to which one can become inordinately attached. Jesus told the rich young man that, if he wanted to be perfect, he should get rid of all his possessions, then come, follow him. Jesus saw some kind of value in poverty, whether deliberately chosen or due to circumstances beyond one's control. What those who are poor by necessity need to recognize is that, while they are not to be discouraged from trying to better their lot, if they accept their involuntary poverty or physical afflictions with the devotion with which the renunciate adopts a life of voluntary poverty, they have already taken the first step toward finding true contentment and happiness which, in the final analysis, is inseparable from finding the God who hides from the proud and the powerful.

There are, of course, impoverished and physically afflicted men and women who so resent what they regard as the injustice of their plight and the way God seems to hide that they turn away from God and even curse the One whom they hold ultimately responsible for their misery. This then becomes their form of hiding from God, in the sense that deep and unresolved resentments throw up a screen against the very possibility of the Light penetrating their darkness. In other words, the poor, too, for reasons of their own — ones emotionally grounded — can cut themselves off from God as effectively as the complacent rich usually do.

We all need to examine the way we respond to our blessings and handicaps. Cursing the darkness never created a flicker of light, and riding mindlessly the crest of a wave of temporal prosperity never brought anyone closer to God. And that, after all, is the only thing that really matters.

Our Culture's Assault on Human Dignity

God is far more hidden in the type of trash culture we live in than in simpler times. The media hawk violence, provide exhausting sensual stimuli, and offer "instant" everything. The "nerd" is apt to be one who, in the mind of the Now Generation, is capable of postponing immediate gratification for the sake of a higher good. The spirit is battered by so much psychic noise that not a sound can get through from the transcendent order. To call attention to this is not to be a chronic spoilsport. The flashing lights and deafening boom of the disco symbolize admirably the nervous, jagged inability of an overstimulated population to be quiet long enough to hear the distant silvery whisper of Lord Krishna's flute. Saturating the senses with kaleidoscopic visual images and the cacophony of ear-splitting noise in the name of art and music is blasphemy against the life of the spirit. The cult of the ugly is guaranteed to hide the soul from God and from itself.

Of course, there is violence in nature, from wind and sea, earthquake and volcano, mudslide and avalanche. The wonder is that in a solar system where the level of heat is totally hostile to any kind of life on Mercury and Venus and near absolute zero on the satellites of the outer planets, and where the raging gaseous storms on fast rotating Jupiter are inconsequential compared with the flaming ball of fire that is our local star, or sun, whose violent nuclear reactions produce a heat that is almost cold compared with the energy released in the explosion of a single stellar nova — I say, the wonder is that by comparison our earth is an unbelievably tranquil place.

Think of the silent morning fogs that glide in from the sea over San Francisco, noiselessly creeping on soft cat feet. See how unpretentiously a rose holds the cool morning dew on its velvet petals, how tall trees grow in silence until they can finger the overarching sky, how snowflakes

sift down to rest on the embracing earth, how life grows noiselessly in
the womb until one feels the developing human begin to stir and seek
the light. All gestation, they say, takes place in the dark. So it is with
the contemplative who carries the hidden God in darkness, in a cloud of
unknowing, awaiting the fullness of time, when the pregnant soul will
bring to light and see face to face what had always been stirring in the
inmost recesses of its being.

Nature reveals the two hands of God: power and peace. If in nature
we see the left and the right hand of God, the divine strength and gen-
tleness, Jesus comes to us as the epitome of these qualities. His "mighty
works," from his healings to calming the storm at sea, are meant to
manifest the power of God as Author of nature, while the meek and
humble Lamb of God reveals God's tranquil beauty. The same Jesus
who stood up against hypocrisy and called those who practiced it white-
washed sepulchers and a brood of vipers, also invited all who were
weary and laboring under heavy burdens to come to him for rest, "For
my yoke is easy, and my burden light" (Matt. 11:30).

In Mark's Gospel, Jesus is at pains to keep a low profile. He seems
to prefer to hide himself and his credentials. After a miraculous cure, he
will disappear into the crowd, and he repeatedly tells those he has healed
to tell no one how it was done but return home and give glory to God.
Here he is a bit like the Beloved in the Song of Solomon who appears
and then in a flash is suddenly gone. He is unwilling to call attention to
himself, even when, out of compassion, he cures a leper or gives sight
to the blind.

The Quickening of Desire

We are all acquainted with the old saw that "absence makes the heart
grow fonder." The seeker cannot avoid wanting to see the absent beloved. His or her very absence makes the interior presence of the form
of the absent person more demanding, more painful. Anyone who has
ever enjoyed a lively sense of the presence of God or of Christ hungers
for a renewed experience of that presence. St. Paul tells us in several
places that he has actually seen Jesus, or that he has seen "the glory of
God in the face of Christ" (1 Cor. 9:1; 15:8; 2 Cor. 4:6). He explains
why he so avidly desires to see Christ again. For we, beholding the glory
of the Lord, "are changed into his likeness" (2 Cor. 3:18). As Plato had
said, we become like what we desire and love.

This "looking on Jesus" (Heb. 12:2) serves to imprint his image on us, so that we become images of the Image of God. Contemplating a painting of the face and figure of Christ can be a catalyst which awakens in us the interior presence of the one we contemplate as an exterior object. But ideally the exterior image should cease to be exterior to us, so that the distinction between object and subject grows thin and eventually evaporates. This describes the pinnacle of the mystical state, the one Paul spoke about in Second Corinthians, referring to the rapture he had experienced fourteen years earlier (2 Cor. 12:2–4).

But that was fourteen years ago. Over the intervening years amid suffering and toil, Paul had to feed on the memory of that ecstatic moment. He did not always live in this Third Heaven but had to "walk by faith." While he is "still in the tent," he groans, longing for the full vision that will never end. To this end he would gladly be dissolved in order to be permanently with Christ. And while far from contemplating self-slaughter, he could easily sympathize with Hamlet in wishing that "this too too solid flesh would melt, thaw, and resolve itself into dew!" (act I, scene ii).

Thus, even among those who have been blessed with the loftiest, ecstatic experiences, there comes a time when they must return to ordinary life. This Monday morning return need not interrupt the sense of an ongoing union with God, but what had been a vision in vivid color is now reduced to a pale gray tracing of the original experience. God is there but will be partially hidden as long as we are enclosed in this "tent." Having revealed his true identity as the Light of the World and as the One Who Is, the author of the Fourth Gospel tells us that Jesus hid himself following each manifestation (John 8:59; 12:36).

The two episodes are almost certainly included to teach us that Jesus as the image of God hides after having granted both material and spiritual favors. As for those who have no faith in him, he says, "You will search for me, but you will not find me; and where I am you cannot come" (John 7:34). God does not reveal the divine self to everyone, even though that Self may dwell within each living soul. God is a hidden God, an elusive Suitor. Only those who seek God first and above everything else can hope to find the Bridegroom. One can appreciate the tenacity of the bride in the Song of Solomon, who says of her beloved: "When I found him whom my soul loves, I held him, and would not let him go" (Song 3:4). But in the World, as long as one is in the body, that is, in the world of impermanence, the Beloved will come and go. Only in eternity will the marriage be consummated, so that we become one spirit with God in uninterrupted joy.

Chapter 9

THE VOICE OF THE BELOVED

Most people are familiar with the story about Mary Magdalene, who came to the tomb in which Jesus had been buried and found it empty. She is greeted there by two angels, who ask her why she is weeping. She answers saying, "They have taken my Lord away and I don't know where they have laid him" (John 20:13). Turning around she sees someone she takes to be a gardener. It is Jesus, but she does not recognize him, at least not until he calls her by name. "Mary," he says. Just "Mary." And immediately she recognizes the voice and the way he used to call her when he was alive. But he is alive, and she can feast her eyes on his radiant risen countenance.

This is not the only postresurrection story in which the disciples of Jesus fail at first to recognize him. We have a similar story when Luke tells us about the two disciples on their way out of the city of Jerusalem walking along the road toward the town of Emmaus. The risen Jesus joins them and walks with them. They discuss at some length the tragic events of the past few days when Jesus was arrested, tried, and crucified. The two disciples still fail to recognize who it is they are speaking with, even though their hearts are warmed as he speaks and explains to them why it was so important that the Messiah suffer and die. Only as they sit together for an evening meal do they recognize him "in the breaking of the bread." Suddenly their eyes are opened and in that very moment he disappears from their sight.

Somewhat later, the Gospel of John has an account of Jesus appearing in Galilee. Seven of his disciples are fishing on the Lake of Galilee. Jesus is standing on the shore, and he tells them where to cast their nets to have a successful catch. They do as told and net a huge number of fish. Only then do they realize that the man on the shore who was giving them fishing lessons was Jesus.

What mysterious, arcane thing are the evangelists trying to tell us by repeatedly informing us that even Jesus' closest friends failed at first to recognize him after his death and resurrection? Judas recognized him even in the dark when he came to the Garden of Gethsemane to betray him. There was a full moon, of course, and that may have helped. But the two disciples who met Jesus on the road to Emmaus met him in broad daylight; the sun was already risen when the disciples finally recognized Jesus standing on the shore of the lake, and the same was true when Mary met Jesus outside his tomb in the cemetery garden.

Do we recognize Jesus in the crotchety old woman next door, in the crack-damaged child of a mother on drugs, even — dare we say it — in our politicians: aldermen, governors, president? God hides. God assumes strange disguises, like a gardener or a garbage man, a stranger out for a walk, an old friend who knows where the fish are. The prophet Isaiah wrote: "Truly you are a hidden God" (Isa. 45:15), and the Psalmist pleads with God, "Hide not yourself" (Ps. 55:1).

In the previous chapter, I called attention to the two occasions when Jesus, after revealing his true identity, "hid himself." There was also a third, earlier occasion when, after healing the paralyzed man at the pool with five porticoes, he "disappeared into the crowd" (John 5:13). The same reticence turns up in Mark's Gospel. After curing a blind man or a leper, he sternly orders the fortunate one to go home and not say anything to anyone about how the healing took place or who was responsible for it.

Jesus, as the image of God working in time, simply will not force himself on anyone. You could meet him in the street and never recognize him. Even if you did, he might say, "Tell no man. Go home and let this visitation be just between the two of us."

Mary Magdalene is a prototype of the contemplative soul with whom God seems to play hide and seek. Like the bride in the Canticle, she seeks the absent one she loves and cannot find him. God does not wear his love for us on his sleeve. We have to long for his embrace, seek him amid the shadows, behind the latticework. And yet he is always present in our inmost self, as that very self, longing for himself in us. You would not seek me had you not already found me. There is no desire for the unknown. To seek God is already to know him though some of us do seek God in strange ways.

Magdalene is seeking the one she loves, yet does not recognize him standing right in front of her. Then he says, "Mary," and the whole world changes. This is the great breakthrough. It can happen to anyone. Think of St. Paul. He stones Stephen and goes out in pursuit of the followers of Jesus to capture them and put them in chains. Then he hears the Voice, "Saul, Saul, why do you persecute me?" Paul had been arresting and binding in chains Jesus. But he did not recognize him. Not until Jesus spoke his name, "Saul, Saul." Or "Jane, Jane . . . Fred, Michael, Eleanor."

One evening Jesus was out under the night sky with his disciples and he pointed to the stars and said, "Do you not know that your names are written in heaven?" Oh, yes, in the heart of God.

What's in a name? Does any one of us really know the name God calls us by? At the Last Supper, Jesus said to his apostles, "I will no longer call you servants but friends." "Amigos." It sounds better in Spanish. You see, the names we go by are only disguises. Only God knows our real eternal name. What I mean is that only God knows us thoroughly and loves us thoroughly. Each one of us is so unique and individual before God that no one else shares our name, just as no one else shares our fingerprints or DNA.

Most people would normally feel flattered or at least pleased if some public figure, someone regularly in the news, knew their name and were able to call them by that name. If a student is falling asleep in class, just let the teacher call her name and she will wake up with a start. This would not happen if someone else's name were being called. What roused Mary Magdalene from her despondent lethargy was the sound of her name as Jesus whispered it softly. Lazarus, too, was awakened from the sleep of death when Jesus stood before his tomb and called out his name, this time in a loud voice, "Lazarus! Lazarus, come forth!" And he did. He responded to the voice of the one who knew his name. When Jesus speaks of himself as the Good Shepherd, he calls his sheep by name. "And the sheep hear his voice. He calls his own sheep by name and leads them out" (John 10:3). To be led out is to be given freedom. The sheep who heard the voice of Jesus and followed him were led into the wide-open spaces, no longer cooped up in a narrow enclosure. That is what hearing the voice of God can do. If we really hear that voice calling our name, then we will be free, and really know who we are, that is, knowing ourselves as God knows us. In that day we shall know, says St. Paul, "even as we are known" (1 Cor. 13:12).

Does God Speak to Us?

Televangelist Pat Robertson says that God talks to him. Maybe he means that he gets ideas and inspirations that seem to come from elsewhere, from somebody else. But is God somebody else? The imagery behind this kind of understanding is that God is a finite being who lives outside us and communicates by some kind of spiritual shortwave system. It is more theologically correct to say that God is nowhere in particular because God is everywhere at once, somewhat as the soul or animating principle of the organism is in every living organ and tissue of the body. Therefore, let us say that God is not elsewhere nor is God somebody else. *Intimior intimo meo,* more profoundly me than my most personal self, expresses St. Augustine's view of the presence of God in the soul.

"O that today you would listen to his voice!" (Ps. 95:7; Heb. 3:7). The voice comes from within, not from without. Its most unmistakable and universal utterance takes the form of the voice of conscience. Elijah heard it as a thin, small voice, less even than a whisper. It was, as the new translation has it, the voice of silence (1 Kings 19:12, NRSV). But it speaks "with most miraculous organ," for we know in our heart of hearts that we should obey what our conscience is telling us, even if it involves the loss of life and property. Henry David Thoreau went to jail for refusing to pay taxes to support what he regarded as an unjust war, and in Second Maccabees a mother and seven of her sons chose cruel deaths rather than violate their own consciences (2 Macc. 7:1–41). Of course, it is always possible to have an erroneous conscience. Jesus warns his disciples that "an hour is coming when those who kill you will think that by doing so they are offering worship to God" (John 16:2). Even so orthodox a theologian as Thomas Aquinas says that one should obey a right conscience, though it might bring one into conflict with ecclesiastical authority. One should, of course, endeavor with every means available to cultivate a right or correct conscience. But in moral matters, it is not always possible to have absolute or metaphysical certitude. With earnest prayer and discernment, however, what is done in good faith cannot be morally reprehensible.

What I am saying in all the above is that, throughout the day in matters great and small, God speaks to us through the light of conscience. Obedience is not always easy, and we can always rationalize noncompliance when the call of duty or charity requires great sacrifice. Most of the time we are only called on to make choices in matters as trivial as offering a kindness to a stranger, holding a door open for an elderly person, driving one's car with care, and offering others the courtesy of the road. Such acts become habitual and second nature for those who practice them regularly. This means that one's conscience — which can be interpreted either as the will of God or more colorfully as the voice of God — is speaking to us. Not just occasionally but always, almost from moment to moment.

I take it on faith that there are some people whose conscience literally speaks to them. They actually hear a voice which they interpret as God's. Promptings of that nature are much less reliable than a clear intelligent understanding of what one ought to do. There are such things, according to the mystics, as substantial words spoken to the deepest reaches of the soul. They are powerful, transforming words; that is, they effect what they say and alter the course of one's life. St. Paul heard such words when the risen Jesus spoke to him and called him by name. But for the rest of his life, he had to respond to the promptings of the Holy Spirit and be guided by the delicate intimations he received that inclined him to one course of action rather than another. God did not tell him in so many words what to do. He had to make crucial decisions based on the few indications that were available to him.

Doing What the Father Does

Jesus, too, had to respond to what he regarded as the will or "voice" of his Father. At times he was strongly impelled to act in a certain way. Mark says that after Jesus' baptism by John, "the Spirit immediately *drove* him out into the wilderness" (Mark 1:12). On other occasions, Jesus came to a decision only after prayer, as when he chose his twelve apostles. Again, when he learned that Herod Antipas, who had killed the Baptist, was inquiring about him, he decided to leave Herod's territory and visit the region in Lebanon around Sidon and Tyre and then cross over to the Syrian district near Caesarea Philippi, not very far from Damascus.

In John's Gospel, Jesus does not say that the Father speaks to him but that he does "only what he sees the Father doing" (John 5:19). I think that the Father is his deeper Self from which he receives a kind of mute "instruction" (John 8:28), so that he always does the things that please the Father. In more philosophical language, Jesus searches within himself to discern the most righteous course to follow and the best one in view of his vocation. Scanning the horizon of what is deepest within him, he guides his life on what he finds there. So he can say, "The Father and I are one.... The Father is in me and I am in the Father" (John 10:30, 38). His elicited, human will is in complete accord with the will of his deeper Self.

That complete accord is tested in the Garden of Gethsemane when Jesus, humanly speaking, shies away from the suffering that awaits him. He prays, "Father, if it is possible, let this cup pass from me" (Matt. 26:39). If not, then let it be. Here he might well have repeated the very same words his own mother spoke when the angel of the annunciation spoke to her: "Let it be with me according to your word" (Luke 1:38).

Human life is replete with opportunities to say, "Let it be." Taking care of an aged parent can be a difficult task for a daughter who has to work and also care for a family. The other brothers and sisters may wiggle out of assuming the responsibility, but that does not excuse the dutiful daughter who does not excuse herself because the others are remiss. She sees what the Father is doing, and she does in like manner. In other words, her conscience instructs her on how to act. That is the way God "speaks" to her. But you have to listen to that thin, small voice that is less than a whisper, yet full of meaning.

We do not always do the things that please the Father, and our conscience may nag us for failing to obey. Holiness consists in being like the shadow that follows and obeys every gesture made by the hand that casts it. Can the shadow refuse to obey the movements of the hand and wander off somewhere on its own? A shadow without the hand is just darkness, night. Those who consistently violate their better instincts walk in their own darkness. But of course there is no darkness that a tiny light cannot swallow and overcome.

The Fourth Gospel presents Jesus as the Light of the World, "the true light which enlightens everyone" (John 1:9). What enlightens us is that in us which shows us the way. You can call it the Father or Jesus, who is both Light and Way, or the Holy Spirit. All together, they constitute the indwelling Holy Trinity. In less theological language, what illumines the way for us is what philosophers call practical reason, not just the practical reason which guides us on how to get things done efficiently, but prudence in moral matters, tact in dealing charitably with others, wisdom in leading a life dedicated to goodness and truth. Deeper still than practical reason and conscience is consciousness itself, which is the human participation in divine illumination, God's light shining in us to endow us with intelligence, free choice, and the ability to judge.

Obeying the Light

When one speaks of seeing what the Father is doing or hearing what God is telling us, we are using visual and auditory symbols to express metaphorically the fact that we do not act without consulting the internal guidance system within us that monitors our actions and establishes the criteria for upright behavior. Though we are occasionally in doubt about what to do, we are not without external helps that come to us from the community. Aside from the fact that religious people can look to scripture, tradition, and the teachings of their particular church, we all should be willing to consult others, counsellors and spiritual guides, to learn what God may be telling us. But again it is worth reminding ourselves that neither Peter, Paul, nor even Jesus himself was given precise instruction by voice mail concerning what they were supposed to do in perplexing circumstances. They had reason to guide them and personal integrity to prevent them from choosing to do what was sinful. But when Jesus decided that the time had come for him to go to Jerusalem, he did not go there because the Father had told him to go and get himself killed in order to redeem the human race. The decisive element was his determination to do as the prophets had done before him. Some were killed and others risked their lives in attacking institutionalized evil, oppression, and the presumptions of the rich and powerful. Jesus died, gave up his life, obeying the light that was in him.

Whenever we see the word "obedience" in the New Testament, we, as freedom-loving Americans, may shudder. It sounds so demeaning, as though we were children. The word does not mean that at all. It means a free response to the appeal of an illumined conscience. It means accepting responsibility for one's actions. Jesus was obedient to his inner daemon. If it led him to the cross, then let it be, let it be! In Hebrews, we are told that "he learned obedience through what he suffered" (5:8), or we might also say that he practiced obedience because "he humbled himself and became obedient to the point of death, even death on a cross" (Phil. 2:8). He followed through. If by some fluke he had not been crucified but lived on to be eighty before ascending into heaven, his obedience would have been just as precious and equally salvific.

Talking to God

Talking is a form of communication, but it is not the only way people communicate. They do it by gesture, the printed word, signals, music, art. God speaks to us through events, through reason, through conscience, through sickness and death. We speak to God every time we perform a good action in response to a person's need or in response to the inner promptings of conscience. We are saying yes to the values which God esteems, being thus of one mind with the Father, doing only the things that please the Father.

Vocal prayer, spoken aloud or whispered interiorly, is first of all a way of acknowledging the existence and reality of God in our lives. It is the feedback or echo of God's speaking to us. The words are less important than the feeling, tone, or manner in which they are offered.

Contemplative prayer, without words, images, or concepts, is a lifting of the mind and heart to God in an attitude of praise, thanksgiving, or adoration. Attitudes speak louder than words. Among the most comprehensive ways of relating to God is through gratitude. Gratitude first of all for the fact of life. Gratitude for the immortality which our spirit shares with God. But there is a gratitude that is generic, nonspecific, not tied down to any single benefit or blessing. It is just a generalized welling up of love, a thanks-for-everything, unspecified gratitude. It gives wings to the soul, and it begins to partake of the boundlessness of God. It elevates the spirit above all that is finite and all but fuses with or dissolves into God.

In the prayer of union, ordinary talking would be a desecration. One simply con-spires, breathes together, with God. This is the highest degree of communion. It is the spiritual marriage, not two in one flesh, but God and the soul become one spirit. If out of the silence one should hear one's name spoken, it would not be simply one's given name. Our name that is written in heaven may be God's own Name. And that is not so strange since, after all, we are "born of God, "offspring of the Most High." Why should we not also bear the Family Name, along with our heavenly God-given name?

When one speaks of being "fused with" God or "dissolving into God," as I just did, this may communicate the erroneous impression that one loses all individuality, like a drop of rain that is absorbed into the ocean and forfeits its identity. True, we may inherit the divine Family Name, but we also retain our own personal name, so that we have two names, one divine and one human, though God-given. What I am saying is that even in the most intimate and highest degree of communion, you do not cease to be you. I do not claim to have this on divine authority, but I do think our passage through time would be senseless if, upon returning to God, we lost all sense of individual personhood and were simply recycled back into the boundless infinite.

The following lines, entitled "The Burning Bush," took shape during a quiet period a few years ago. The thought is not original since it clearly depends on the Song of Solomon in the Bible and on the poetry of St. John of the Cross. However, it does bring together some of the ideas touched on in the last three chapters.

> When I was a child
> I saw the glare of brash sunlight on a loveless earth,
> The sad light of long afternoons,
>   And knew the emptiness of all created things.

How long the days were,
With hopes for the morrow never realized.
Hungry eyes, inexperienced in disappointment,
Scanned the horizons of desire,
Seeking and failing to find —
   Not knowing that God was walking in my garden.

Bitter joys, these!
No earthly kingdom, not even the whole world
Can fill the hungry heart.
Even then the first faint touch of Your love
Was working deep within:
Bitter-sweet, tender immanence,
That knows not whether to laugh or weep.

There came the soft sift of a melody
As of some fine, far off music,
So dim and faint that one might wonder
Whether it was not the echo of the soul's own silence.
It was a love song full of deep and moving urgency.
Yet my unheeding heart doubted,
   Not knowing that You were walking in my garden.

In solitary moments, unasked, You came.
Your quiet eyes and golden countenance
Pierced through the night,
Luminous in the darkness.

If I should cry in the night for You,
Will you, O Lord, be gone like the mountain hart?
Why do You start at every sound and vanish?

Seal our love in silence,
Lest stirring I wake from love's dream
And the keepers take my veil away.

Now is your cross a column of fire,
The Burning Bush ablaze,
And will not be consumed.
Here is fire's Substance
Hanging torchlike on a tree,
Vivid, livid, deathless love.

Who will salt me with this fire?
Who will purge all self away?

Part Two

THE HUMANITY OF JESUS

Chapter 10

LIKE US, EXCEPT FOR SIN

A recurring theme in the New Testament is that Jesus, though tempted as we are, was nevertheless without sin (John 8:46; 2 Cor. 5:21; Heb. 4:15; 1 Pet. 2:22). How did the evangelists come upon this knowledge? Neither they nor any of the other scripture writers knew Jesus in the flesh, with the possible exception of the Beloved Disciple, who, though he may not have written the Fourth Gospel, is presented as the source for the material found in the Gospel (John 21:24).

First, there is the argument that would have appealed to the first Christians. If in their minds Jesus was the Messiah and universal savior, it would have been highly inappropriate for him to have been a sinner. Secondly, as the inaugurator of the New Covenant between God and humankind, he must have been gifted with a high degree of sanctity. Thirdly, as one who preached holiness and the importance of sinlessness to others, one would expect him to be a model of what he preached. Finally, he is represented in the Gospels as a man of prayer, humble, forgiving — even of Judas whom he called "friend" at the very moment he betrayed him (Matt. 26:50) — and obedient to the will of God.

On the other hand, since the baptism of John the Baptist was a baptism of repentance for sins committed, the fact that Jesus submitted to John's baptism suggests that he thought of himself as qualified to be known as a sinner. Mark's Gospel leaves that impression, though the later evangelists, especially Matthew and John, are at pains to assure us that the Baptist felt unworthy to baptize so privileged a person as Jesus. This was not the judgment of Jesus' enemies. They accused him of being a sinner and a glutton, a winebibber who consorted with sinners. And he was put to death with criminals, which in the eyes of many was sufficient to stigmatize Jesus as an evildoer. Even if he did work miracles, his adversaries were not impressed. The ancient world was peopled with magicians who beguiled the masses with their pseudo-cures. Even if some cures were genuine, they were often thought to be achieved with the help of some malevolent power, such as Beelzebul, the archdevil.

What distinguished Jesus from other healers was that he cured by a word and did not engage in mystification and complicated rituals.[5] Jesus was not a charlatan or a deceiver.

Temptations

The word that is traditionally translated as "temptation" in the Lord's Prayer and elsewhere in the Gospels (*peirasmos*) does not mean an inducement to sin but has the sense of a test, as when a precious metal is cast into the crucible to be tested by fire in order to ascertain its worth or genuineness. Jesus was tempted, say the three Synoptic Gospels. "Then Jesus was led by the Spirit into the wilderness to be tempted by the devil" (Matt. 4:1). Remember how in the Book of Job, Satan (who in that book is not an evil character but a member of the heavenly court whose assignment is to put God's saints to the test to see if they will still honor God in adversity) challenges God to let him test Job: "But stretch out your hand now, and touch all that he has, and he will curse you to your face" (Job 1:11).

The trial or test for true holiness can take either of two forms: The successful person runs the risk of becoming puffed up and power hungry, and in this way falling into sin; or the person may cave in under adversity and "curse God to his face." Jesus underwent both kinds of trials. When he was having enormous success in Galilee, healing the sick and being followed by crowds of admirers, were he like many successful people, he might have been tempted to attribute his success to his own innate ability and misuse the adulation of the masses for his own self-aggrandizement. The desert "temptation" by Satan condenses to forty days the kind of test Jesus could have been subject to during those months when he was the darling of the multitudes. Who needs God when you can work miracles by simply uttering a command? Could one not turn stones to bread, leap down from the pinnacle of the Temple and land unhurt to impress the people, and in this way acquire prestige enough to become ruler not only of Palestine but of the whole world? When a particular rabbi or layperson gains the reputation of being especially holy, other Jewish rabbis and teachers set out to test the reputed saint in order to find out if he is humble and filled with loving kindness toward God and all creatures. They are not so much tempters

---

5. See Morton Smith, *Jesus the Magician* (New York: Barnes and Noble, 1978).

as testers. So Jesus came through Satan's test in the desert with flying colors.

But what about adversity? What if all your friends turn against you and abandon you in your darkest hour? What if one of your disciples betrays you, while another denies that he ever knew you? What if you are falsely accused of criminal activity, summarily tried, scourged, and crucified, while your enemies gloat over your misfortune? Will you "curse God, and die," as Job's wife recommended when misfortune struck her husband? Jesus on the cross did feel as though all had abandoned him, his Father included. But this did not prevent him from praying to that same Father to forgive his enemies. To the end he carried out what he regarded as his Father's will, and he died with a cry of exaltation: *Consummatum est.* The work is done, "I have finished the work that you gave me to do" (John 17:4).

The author of Hebrews says of Jesus that he is "one who in every respect has been tested" (Heb. 4:15), and that "he learned obedience through what he suffered" and was thus "made perfect" (Heb. 5:8). Life is a learning process. If Jesus learned obedience through the things he suffered and by being tested, we, too, are given the opportunity to do the same by life's daily thwartings which, if accepted as gifts on the road to perfection, can be seen as elements in the honing process that refines the soul. Our "obedience" can then be interpreted as a willing acceptance, without resentment, of the ordinary and extraordinary hardships life in the body is subject to.

Saint or Sinner

St. Paul was accustomed to address his letters to the saints (*hagioi*) in Rome or Corinth or at Ephesus. Not that all were saints, but the vocation of all was to be on the holiness track. Most of those who are apt to pick up this book will be people who are doing their best to make the optimum use of the capital with which they have been endowed. If they are inclined to judge themselves severely, this is usually because they are conscientious and have high ideals. Looking back over their younger years, they may be appalled by what they now judge to have been the insensitivity they showed in those early days. Even now they may be disappointed with their inability to measure up to the standard they have set for themselves. Paradoxically, awareness of failure is a sure sign of success. It means that one is not obtuse and blind to one's shortcomings. Jesus warned those who blindly prided themselves on their holiness: "But now that you say, 'We see,' your sin remains" (John 9:41).

The ideal lies somewhere between scrupulosity, which is seeing sin where there is none, and complacency, which chooses either to ignore one's faults or shrug them off as of no consequence. Even the greatest among the saints have their faults, but they are not necessarily sinful faults. Did Jesus have any faults? The evangelists were certainly agreed on not mentioning them, in case they did exist. But Jesus, as a human being and like us in all things, was certainly fallible. He could make mistakes, as he did in choosing Judas as an apostle. He could stumble or stub his toe, grow weary and contract a cold, attribute to demons simple physical afflictions, such as leprosy or epilepsy. To be without sin does not mean to be without human faults.

Is it conceivable that other human beings, in spite of their faults, can also have lived lives free from sin? What children do, before the cerebral cortex of the brain is fully developed, should not be written off immediately as sinful. A baby in discomfort can be cranky. A youth seeking to find himself may overcompensate for a sense of insecurity and seem arrogant or insubordinate. But remember: at every stage of our lives, the saying still holds, "God isn't finished with me yet." Another popular version holds, "It ain't over till its over." Each one's *consummatum est* cannot be uttered until one breathes one's last.

I would not be shocked to learn that Jesus had some faults. As a child, it does seem that he was inconsiderate of his parents when he disappeared from their sight at the age of twelve and caused them a great deal of anguish by not informing them about where he was. Mary put it straight to him: "Child, why have you treated us like this? Look, your father and I have been searching for you in great anxiety" (Luke 2:48). Or one might wonder whether it was really necessary for Jesus to insult the Syrophoenician woman, who only asked for a favor, by saying that "it is not fair to take the children's food and throw it to the dogs," implying that she, a Gentile woman, was a dog (Mark 7:27). No doubt, a spiritual lesson is attached to all these stories. Jesus may only have been testing the faith of those he dealt with, but on the face of it some of his actions seem to be at least discourteous. And there was little courtesy in Jesus' action when he made a scourge and drove out the money-changers from the Temple and scattered their coins all over the area. He must have been very angry to resort to such an act of violence. But anger, of itself, is not sinful. Far from being a fault, righteous anger is in order when one is faced with a truly outrageous situation.

There is enough sin in the world to convince the most optimistic that there is no crime so horrendous that some human beings will not commit it. But, while it can be debated whether the vast majority of people are basically good, there are now and have always been extremely holy and just men and women, people whose faults and imperfections are so insignificant that they are like the rest of us in all other respects, sin alone excluded. The church's mission is, of course, to encourage people to lead upright lives. Unfortunately, the message of Jesus as preached over the centuries has been so overlaid with sin and guilt that the general impression is communicated that everyone is innately sinful. John Calvin held that as a result of the sin of Adam human nature was rotten to the core. Even newborn babies were steeped in sin. But the church, mandated by Christ, has the remedy. If you're selling a cure for snakebite, you should first convince potential customers that they have been bitten. Failing that, be ready to supply a dutiful snake whose bite will justify their buying your spiritual antidote.

No doubt, some people need to be convinced of sin — their own — but most of us are helped more by encouragement than by condemnation. So much depends on the intention motivating an act. In Jesus' day the School of Shammai took a rigorist stand, preferring to characterize an act as good or bad depending on the results, independent of the intention of the agent. Pious people today often blame themselves for something they could not help, whether due to an accident or an innocent oversight. In spite of shortcomings, I am convinced that many people lead blameless lives. Even if they have faults and occasionally do things they regret, I do not think these "venial" lapses offend God.

But what if I keep trying and still cannot overcome a fault which others find offensive? Sometimes one has to learn to tolerate what amounts to a temperament or character defect, the latter being more serious than the former. In that case one has to learn to live with and forgive oneself. In the ideal order, it would be better if everyone were nice. Meanwhile, we should put up with one another, bearing one another's burdens (Gal. 6:2), being slow to judge the intentions of others, knowing that we, too, with the best will in the world cannot overcome some of our faults. If we readily excuse others, then we will be excused. This is the import of the petition in the Lord's Prayer: "Forgive us our faults, as we have also forgiven others for their faults." Forgiveness of others comes first, but when that is done, our own faults will be found to weigh lighter on the scales of justice and mercy.

Self-Respect

When pressed to declare *who* he was, Jesus did not lay claim to any exalted title or description. He was simply the generic, anonymous "Son of Man." Or, in John's Gospel, he was just "I am" without description. We, on the other hand, seek to define ourselves in terms of race, nationality, family, religion, titles, possessions, age, sex, and so on. And of course in this world we have to be some *where* and some *how*. But these designations do not adequately express our ultimate *who*. As I will indicate at some length in chapter 15, we are made in God's own image as immortal beings, participants in the divine life. The fully actualized person does not seek to identify with any quality, with any of what Beatrice Bruteau calls "descriptions."[6] These are the finite, accidental attributes we acquire in the course of embodiment. At the root of our being we are not any of our descriptions, those tags we wear in public or even in the privacy of our self-imaging. We simply are an *I am*.

In John's Gospel, the formless, indescribable *I am* is also the Son of Man. What is true of the theandric Jesus as the archetype or model of incarnation is also true, with distinction, of every human person. But, it can be argued in protest, he was without sin. True, but also like us in every other respect. Among those respects, I would include his theandric nature. Being without sin does not ipso facto assign him to another species, thus making it impossible for others to follow him and model themselves on his example. And since I do not regard ordinary, involuntary faults and failings as an offense against God, therefore as "sins" in the traditional sense, I think that others, both Christians and non-Christians, can eventually come to lead sinless lives. This will not sit well with those who are committed to holding that the sin of an original legendary pair has so infected all members of the human race, like a contagious disease, that it is impossible for anyone to be conceived and be born without sin, let alone lead blameless lives.

Looking around at the heinous crimes committed by some members of the human race, it is easy to conclude to the total corruption of all. But the range of good and evil covers an enormously broad spectrum, from the angelic to the demonic. The first thing to note is that while sinlessness opens a chasm between a sinless person and the rest of humankind, of itself this does not mean that the metaphysical structure of saint and sinner is different. Jesus was born and grew up to mature

---

6. See "The Descriptive Self," in *Radical Optimism* (New York: Crossroad, 1993), 77ff.

manhood like anyone else in his culture. He was tempted, frustrated, wearied, in need of food and shelter, was vulnerable and eventually killed by his enemies. As for the exalted titles with which others honored him, the only two he seems to have applied to himself were the two mentioned at the start of this section: the naked "I am," stressing his divinity beyond all descriptions, and "Son of Man," indicating his integral humanity and solidarity with all human beings. It is true that the evangelists and other New Testament writers apply to him majestic and royal titles — "descriptions" — to confess their faith in his uniqueness. One can hardly quarrel with their belief in that uniqueness. In their experience there was no one quite like him, and while belief in his divinity grew over the four or five decades following his death and resurrection, that belief was grounded in the final understanding of who he was. The next step, which his followers took only gradually, was the belief that those who believed in his name became children of God, born not of the flesh but of God. But they did not take the further step and allow that all those created in the image of God, which is everybody, not just Christians, are divine offspring. Exclusivism is hard to overcome.

No one who vividly realizes what being the image of God or a divine offspring implies can fail to have deep respect for themselves and for others. People who have a poor self-image need to be told not only that God loves them but that they are royalty, scions of the Most High, born of God. Once convinced of this identity, *noblesse oblige*. One will gain self-respect, begin to act the part, and achieve a degree of holiness no sermon about loathsome human sinfulness could hope to provoke.

Standing the Test

Jesus was tempted, that is, tested in prosperity and in what appeared to be gross misfortune. He did not yield an inch, but grew in stature because of the pressures he was subjected to and overcame. Our little inconspicuous lives do not have to face the ordeal Jesus had to undergo. But from birth to death we suffer annoyances, have to make painful decisions, to adjust to the death of our dearest relatives and friends. Not to buckle, even when one cannot hold back tears, is what the example of Jesus is telling us. He has revealed what the human is capable of. If you think you are worthless and have all but given up trying, try to remember *who* you are. Jesus knew who he was and that was the source of his strength. He could face a most cruel death because he knew that he was immortal. Those who are convinced that this life is all there is

ought to despair or go insane when fortune's heavy hand afflicts them
in body, mind, or possessions. Very often life reserves the most painful
and humiliating episodes to the last few years or months of one's earthly
existence. Can one stand the test?

Some people cannot even stand prosperity. It can be the greatest test
of all, as one's integrity is probed. Power corrupts. Wealth can lead to,
if it does not stem from, greed. Temporal success can induce a forgetfulness of eternity. Very often the very kindest thing that life can do for
heady plutocrats is to cause their house of cards to come tumbling down
upon their heads, as they lose health, wealth, the respect of others, and
social position. What no one would have wished for is often the best
spiritual medicine.

We have to learn to take our spiritual ups and downs in stride, seeing
our trials, tests, temptations as opportunities, and not panic when the
worst happens. We cannot block out our feeling, nor should we. What
sweetens the most bitter disappointments is the conviction that our inheritance is eternal life. And that means much more than the survival of
the death of the organism. It means entering into the glory of God, no
longer asleep in the latent state we were in before coming into the world,
but awake and fully conscious of sharing in the divine manner of being
with untold numbers of saints drawn from every nation under the sun.

Chapter 11

THE HUMILITY OF JESUS

Mark's is the shortest of the four Gospels, and most scholars regard it as the earliest. Matthew and Luke depend upon it, often using almost the same wording, while rearranging some of the borrowed material. The Fourth Gospel is cut from a different cloth, though at times it does join the other three in a number of incidents and in parts of the passion narrative. The other Gospels do add material not found in Mark, but this comes by way of addition to their primary source.

An important conclusion to be drawn from the partial dependence of the other Gospels on Mark is that the portrait Mark paints of Jesus is more primitive and closer to the Jesus of history. While the other Gospels add passages that glorify Jesus until, in the Fourth Gospel, he is presented as divine and actually claiming divinity, Mark's Jesus is meek and humble of heart. He makes no personal claims for himself, and he seems throughout his public ministry to be trying to keep a low profile. He almost seems to be embarrassed by the fame his miracles occasion. If Jesus thought he was the promised Messiah, it was a secret he kept to himself. In fact, this reticence has been called "the messianic secret." Only under oath, when standing before Caiaphas the high priest, does Jesus answer "I am" to the question, "Are you the Messiah?" (Mark 14:61). In answer to the same question, however, Jesus does not give an affirmative answer in Matthew and Luke, but throws the question back on Caiaphas with the enigmatic, "You say" (*su eipas*). In other words, he does not say that he is the Messiah, though Caiaphas might say so and go on to condemn Jesus for blasphemy on the basis of something the high priest had in mind or had heard from someone else. We get an insight on this kind of answer in the Fourth Gospel when Pilate asks Jesus whether or not he claims to be the King of the Jews. Jesus answers with a "*You* say" reply: "Do you ask this on your own, or did others tell you about me?" (John 18:34). To a direct question about his identity or personal claims, Jesus leaves it for others to decide.

When Jesus does speak of himself, most often he avoids the use of the first-person pronoun, but refers to himself as the nondescript and neutral "Son of Man." In Matthew's later Gospel, Jesus does not hesitate to declare, "You have heard it said,... but *I* say to you," seeming to be quite willing to assert his authority alongside that of Moses, who gave the Ten Commandments. Mark's Jesus, by contrast, does not set himself over against earlier authorities. He came to fulfill, not to annul, the Torah.

Your Faith Has Made You Well

If, out of compassion, Jesus works a miracle, the one who is healed must not publicize his or her good fortune nor even attribute it to Jesus. To the woman who was healed of a flow of blood, Jesus declares, "Your faith has made you well." He says the same thing to blind Bartimaeus, attributing the man's recovery of his sight to his faith (Mark 10:52). Earlier, a deaf man had been cured of his affliction. Those who witnessed the miracle were not to publicize it. "And he charged them to tell no one" (John 7:36). In Mark 5:19, Jesus, after pacifying a wild man who lived outside the town in the hills among the tombs, told the man to go home to his house and not linger with Jesus. A solemn admonition was given to a healed leper: "See that you say nothing to anyone, but go, show yourself to the priest" (Mark 1:44). When a man possessed by an evil spirit cried out, "I know who you are, the Holy One of God," Jesus rebuked him and commanded him to be silent (1:25, 34). In the Fourth Gospel there are instances of the same shyness about publicity. The invalid whom Jesus cured at the pool of Bethesda did not know who his benefactor was (John 5:13). So also in the ninth chapter. The blind man to whom Jesus had restored his sight apparently did not know who had healed him until Jesus later found him and revealed himself (John 9:37).

During his lifetime, Jesus' disciples were not to reveal to anyone who they thought he was. When Peter declared that he was the Christ, he and the others were *sternly* forbidden to make any mention of what they believed about him (Mark 8:30). Again, coming down the mountainside after the transfiguration, Peter, James, and John, who had witnessed Jesus' glorification, were "to tell no one what they had seen" until after his death and resurrection (Mark 9:9). Finally, when Jesus restored to life the dead daughter of Jairus, he wanted to do so in private, "in the house." So he put out all the mourners, saying euphemistically that "the child is not dead but sleeping" (5:39). In this way he sought to minimize the miracle.

The Secret Doctrine

If Jesus made a point of hiding his identity, neither did he preach his more elevated, secret doctrine to the multitudes. When he wants to reveal some especially delicate truth to his immediate disciples, he pulls them apart from the crowd and takes them indoors in order to speak to them, as it were, behind closed doors. This is what is called the "in house" doctrine. It is Mark's highly individual way of distinguishing between what Jesus does and says in public and what he says when teaching his special friends in a hidden and secret way. "In the house" means in private, for a chosen few. What is true of the miracles is equally true of Jesus' teaching: "To you has been given the secret of the kingdom of God, but for those *outside* everything is in parables" (4:11).

Jesus was especially eager to impart to his disciples his most profound teachings before he was taken from them. As it became increasingly clear that his days were numbered, he needed to spend more time with them. Passing through Galilee after his transfiguration, Jesus "would have no one know it," for he was using the time to teach his disciples (9:30). We meet again with this desire to escape notice and be alone with his close followers when he leaves Galilee and travels north to the region around Tyre and Sidon. There "he *entered a house,* and would not have anyone know it" (7:21). What he did in the house was, no doubt, instruct his disciples in private.

To be noted is that, even within the inner circle of the twelve, there was a special group of three who were privy to things the others did not witness. Only Peter, James, and John witnessed the transfiguration. The same three were with Jesus in the house when he raised the daughter of Jairus. And they accompanied him during his agony in the garden. The three were party to the ecstasy and the agony, fortified by what they had witnessed on Mt. Tabor for the scandal of the agony and the cross. But in the end they all fled.

Most of the great spiritual teachers have a few carefully chosen disciples who are privileged to hear the master's more advanced doctrine. It would be a waste and unproductive to cast spiritual pearls before crowds of people who were not sufficiently advanced in the spiritual path to appreciate what they were being fed. But the day would come, probably after the death of Jesus, when what had been said in private and done in a hidden way would be made public. "For there is nothing hid, except to be made manifest, nor is anything secret, except to come to light" (4:22). All these things would eventually be made public. But during his earthly life, Jesus preferred the obscurity and anonymity of the "Son of Man."

Needless to say, Jesus could not really have it both ways. No matter how earnestly and severely he impressed on others the importance of keeping silent about his works and identity, so much the more did they broadcast what they had seen and heard. In spite of Jesus' admonition to keep silent about his cure, the man with the withered hand "went out and began to talk freely about [his cure] and to spread the news, so that Jesus could no longer openly teach in a town, but was out in the country, and people came to him from every quarter" (1:45).

Mark gives us an example of the way Jesus explained the deeper meaning of his teaching to his disciples in private. What is it that truly defiles a man? When his disciples failed to understand the answer Jesus had given the crowd, he took them aside and, leaving the crowd outside, he "entered the house" where he explained that what defiles a man is not the kind of food he takes in, something that worried the Pharisees a great deal, but the kind of words and thoughts that come out from him (7:17). And why were his disciples unable to cure the boy suffering from convulsions? "When he entered the house . . . he said to them, 'This kind cannot be driven out by anything but prayer'" (9:29). Or again, it was "in the house" that Jesus explained to his disciples why he regarded a man who repudiated his wife and married another to be an adulterer (10:10).

So whether a person is cured and told to avoid the public eye and go straight to his house, or whether Jesus provides his secret teaching to his disciples "in the house," house is a code word in Mark for helping us understand Jesus, a man who, in spite of his successful public mission, was a private kind of person who did not trumpet his own wares nor seek the cheap publicity of the magician or medicine show operator. In the Fourth Gospel, Jesus' brothers urged him to go up to Jerusalem for the Feast of Tabernacles and work some miracles there. "Show yourself to the world," they said (John 7:4). This episode projects a very Markan note into John's Gospel, a Gospel in which Jesus is not shy about calling attention to his "works" as proof that he has God's approval. In Mark, his conduct is closer to the principles he laid down for others: Avoid ostentation. Do not seek the first place nor the acclaim of men. When you do a good deed, let it "be in secret, and your Father who sees in secret will reward you" (Matt. 6:4). Jesus did go up to Jerusalem for the Feast of Tabernacles, but "he went up not publicly, but privately" (John 7:10).

Failure

People ran after Jesus because of what they thought they could get from him. Jesus, however, was not deceived by the momentary enthusiasm of the masses. "You seek me because you ate your fill of the loaves" (John 6:36). The enthusiasm of the fickle crowd would soon cool when it was learned that Jesus had no intention of challenging their Roman overlords and that he had no political ambitions. A kingdom not of this world was the last thing they were interested in. What they wanted was bread and the circus, food and entertainment. In fact, Jesus almost sees his miracles as an impediment to what he regarded as his proper ministry, which was to teach and convince the world of God's love.

Mark does not disguise the fact that from the start Jesus had to be prepared to face failure. Not only did he fail to win the lasting allegiance of the poor masses, but his own family thwarted him and his townspeople disowned him. They all thought he must be mad when he was mobbed by an unruly crowd (3:21). The scribes who had been sent down from Jerusalem to carry back a report on him declared that he was possessed by a demon (3:22). His closest disciples misunderstood him, failing to grasp the essence of his teaching, vying for first place, trying to interfere with his plans. Eventually, even some of the twelve would deny, doubt, or betray him.

Mark portrays Jesus as being increasingly surrounded by darkening clouds until, abandoned by all, he would hang forlorn on the cross, forsaken by all but the women who followed him to Calvary but stood off at a distance. How can the picture of a man so badly defeated by life's circumstances win the loyalty of others? The answer lies in the fact that Mark and those for whom Mark's Gospel was written claim to know *who* Jesus was beneath his simple outer appearance. And they also know the end of the story. "He is risen," announced the angel of the resurrection to the frightened women. "He is not here; see the place where they laid him" (16:6).

Mark's early Christian converts, whether from Judaism or the Gentile world, could only marvel at the humility and self-effacing character of the one whose greatness transcended every human and angelic category. Unlike the other three Gospels, Mark's Gospel is triumphalism in reverse. But there is another kind of victory, one so hard for ordinary mortals to achieve. It consists in the down-playing of self, the unwillingness to exploit the trust of people for one's own advantage. It is the hiddenness of Jesus that stands out. It is a divine quality. "Truly, you are a God who hides himself," wrote Isaiah (Isa. 45:15). But one does not light a lamp and keep it forever under wraps, under a basket or under the bed (Mark 4:21). For Mark, it was the faith of those who believed in Jesus that was able to penetrate his incognito and see in his darkest moments the majesty of his person, something the other Gospels set out to highlight.

Jesus often forbad those who witnessed his powers and heard his esoteric doctrine to say anything about them until after his death. He was not one to encourage the cult of personality. In political dictatorships, the more despotic the ruler the larger are the statues and images trumpeting his godlike qualities. One thinks of Russia and China under the domination of Stalin or Mao Tse-tung, or Iraq and Iran under their rulers, Islamic countries in which the cult of images is in direct violation of the teaching of the Koran. In the United States, you have to be dead to have your image imprinted on a postage stamp. Of course, one might argue with Jesus' decision to postpone until after his death release of information about his advanced teaching and word about his transfiguration. Wouldn't the apostles forget exactly what he had said or misrepresent it? At least others did do just that. Had Jesus lived to the ripe old age of eighty as did the Buddha or Plato, he might have been able to control better the development of the Christian church. On the other hand, Jesus felt that after his death, "When the Spirit comes, he will guide you into all truth" (John 16:13).

Jesus must have known that he was a man of destiny, quite aside from any infused knowledge he might have been favored with by God. The posthumous Jesus is certainly vastly more renowned than the prophet who walked along the hills and valleys of ancient Palestine. Only the most ignorant people in the remotest parts of the world may never have heard of him, but they are in a definite minority. The fact is that he died in relative obscurity in an obscure province in a despised part of the world as far as the Greeks and Romans were concerned. As he hung taut and dying on the cross, could anyone, even Jesus, have anticipated that human events would be dated as having taken place before or after the presumed date of his birth? Is this the man who in real life sought to escape notice? It was something he tried to achieve, but his love and compassion for the sick and the oppressed betrayed his most heartfelt desire. He could not resist the temptation to succor the needy, cure the sick and the impaired, and in this way become an important public figure. It was that limited notoriety and the crowds he drew that alarmed Caiaphas and Pilate, along with the fact that he had offended too many people who had the power to destroy him. And they lost no time in setting up the machinery to do exactly that.

I think Jesus understood perfectly well from the start how dangerous it is to become famous. People cannot help but notice you, and that
means that you become an object of devotion for some and a target to
be brought down for others. Paul and the later evangelists sought to give
Jesus his due. With each succeeding Gospel and New Testament book,
he is presented in increasingly exalted terms. The rabbi, the teacher, the
prophet becomes Son of David, Messiah, Lord, Son of God. There was
nothing hidden that would not be eventually revealed. So it has been
with so many great artists, musicians, and poets. They remained virtually unknown while in the flesh, or were appreciated only by a few, only
to be recognized as geniuses after their deaths. Jesus somehow knew that
the world would never be quite the same after his passing. But during his
short span of years on earth, he was simply a human being, man's son,
the Son of Man. Let others make of him what they would. He was not
running for any particular office. This is Mark's Jesus. Even in his most
colorful, dramatic moments, when he lashed out at the hypocrisy of the
Pharisees, or multiplied the loaves and fishes, or stampeded the money-
changers and cattle out of the Temple court, Jesus never stayed around
to collect words of praise or blame. He could disappear as quickly as
he had appeared, as he did on a number of occasions when his enemies
were ready to kill him (see Luke 4:29–30; John 8:59).

Who Do People Say That I Am?

On the road to the villages around Caesarea Philippi not far from snow-
capped Mt. Hermon, Jesus put two questions to his disciples. The first
was, "Who do the people say that I am?" and the second, addressed
to his disciples, was, "Who do *you* say that I am?" (Mark 8:27–29).
Setting aside the answers he received to the two questions, we may ask
why Jesus asked them in the first place? Was he uncertain about *who*
he was? Or did he ask in order to find out what his close disciples,
compared with the masses, thought of him? In Matthew's Gospel, Jesus
praises Peter for having concluded that he was the Christ, the expected
Messiah, but this is an embellishment not found in Mark or Luke. All
three Gospels make it clear that Jesus did not want anyone to go about
saying that he was the Messiah. It was, of course, dangerous; for Messiah to some meant king, and king meant rebellion to the Romans. The
"crime" Jesus was crucified for was, in the eyes of Pilate, his being hailed
as "King of the Jews." That was what Pilate caused to be written at the
head of the cross.

I am convinced, however, that Jesus was minimally interested in playing Messiah or claiming for himself that role. It was far too limiting and parochial. John comes closer to the truth in the Fourth Gospel, where Jesus sheds all titles and simply presents himself as a naked "I am," free of all descriptions. True, this is usually interpreted to mean that John was here asserting the divinity of Jesus, since "I am," or *egō eimi,* is the name assigned to God in the Septuagint Version of the Hebrew Bible. I have said that "I am" is the nameless name, the one that also refers to the descriptionless core of every human being. As a designation which can only point to that which is ineffable in each one of us, the "I am" far transcends being king, president, mother, or Messiah. Jesus had a deep sense of his divine filiation as Child of God, and the reality of Jesus escapes finite descriptions and the boundaries of material time and space. The "I am" is "who" Jesus is. That is why he refused to identify with and be owned by the members of his own family, why he rejected ethnic exclusivism and spoke of the Gentiles entering the kingdom and coming to sit down at table with Abraham, Isaac, and Jacob. He would accept nothing so restrictive as Messiah nor so local as a privileged place of worship, whether it be Jerusalem, Rome, or Benares (John 4:21).

So, call him what you will, in the end even Mark, with some effort, has Jesus say to the high priest during his trial, "I am." Caiaphas had asked if he was the Messiah, and in reply Mark's Jesus gives the mysterious answer, which is not a yes but a declaration of his true identity as *egō eimi.* Jesus gives the same kind of response to the Samaritan woman at the well of Jacob in John's Gospel. She says that she knows that when the Messiah comes, he will tell us all the things we need to know. In reply, Jesus does not say, "It is I [the Messiah] who am speaking to you," but simply "I am" is the one who is speaking to you. This statement is contrived in John's Gospel, but the evangelist is deliberately trying to make a point. Jesus is much more than the Messiah. Down the ages the Jews from their point of view have been right in not wanting to call him that. For the Messiah was to usher in an era of lasting peace and prosperity. These blessings have not yet come upon the earth. Jesus, the Jew, would probably agree. In any case, names meant nothing to Jesus, for the ultimate source of his being lay beyond every name and all descriptions.

So he left open the question of who he was, hoping that with time at least some people would manage to get past the limits of sex, nation, ethnicity, and high-sounding titles, not only as applied to himself but as applied to all his true followers. Jesus despised pretense and self-promotion, garments with long fringes, and the idea that you know somebody because you are able to call that person by name or title. So, even in the most public periods of his life, he managed to hide, neither taking credit for his cures nor claiming for himself any finite, earthly title. In this he was truly divine, like the God who hides, referred to in chapter 8.

Chapter 12

HIS UNDERSTANDING OF
THE HUMAN CONDITION

Language purists used to complain about Sir Winston Churchill's habit of ending sentences with one or more prepositions. For example, "Stupidity is one of the things we should not put *up with*." Cherubic, mischievous Winnie offered to correct himself by saying, "Stupidity is the kind of thing *up with which* we should not put."

Reading the Gospels one can only admire and sympathize with Jesus, seeing the kind of stupidity in the apostles "up with which he had to put." Having made it clear over and over again that his "kingdom is not from the world" (John 18:36), we find the apostles still asking him during one of his appearances after the resurrection, "Lord, is this the time when you will restore the kingdom to Israel?" (Acts 1:6). They still failed to understand the kind of kingdom Jesus had been preaching for the weeks and months they had walked with him. When some village Samaritans refused to grant hospitality to Jesus and his disciples, two of them asked, "Lord, do you want us to command fire to come down from heaven and consume them?" (Luke 9:54). Aside from the presumption that these two could actually command thunder and lightning to come down and "consume" the villagers, the episode shows how poorly the two had grasped a central theme of Jesus' program. Violence was totally at variance with his idea of the kingdom. No wonder he called John and James, the two who wanted to destroy the village and its inhabitants, "Sons of thunder," or *boanerges* (Mark 3:17).

On another occasion, the same John tried to stop a man who was not a member of the apostolic band from casting out demons in Jesus' name. "Do not stop him," ordered Jesus. Such a man was not likely to speak against him any time soon (Mark 9:39). It was the same John and James who pulled Jesus aside and asked him to promise them top rank in the kingdom, sitting beside him at his left and right hand. Jesus did promise them a favor, but it was not of the kind they had anticipated. Like the two criminals crucified to the left and the right of Jesus on

Calvary, they would share in his suffering, and in this way also share in his glory (Mark 10:39). Matthew, who wants to spare the two Sons of Thunder from another instance of self-promoting arrogance, says that it was their mother who asked Jesus to grant her sons the favor of sitting at his left and right hand when he came into his glory (Matt. 20:20). Blame it on the woman, Adam!

John and James were not the only two who were not loath to use violence. When the chief priests sent out a substantial band of well-armed men to arrest Jesus, Peter whipped out a sword — he was probably left-handed — and cut off the right ear of Malchus, one of the high priest's slaves (Luke 22:50; John 18:10). Where did Peter get the sword? It must have been one of the two referred to at the end of the Last Supper when several of the disciples, ready to defend Jesus, said, "Lord, look, here are two swords" (Luke 22:38). Two swords against the Temple militia and the whole Roman army! Jesus did not laugh, but his voice must have betrayed frustration as he said, "It is enough." Again, right up to the end they misconstrued the very substance of his message of peace and nonviolence.

So we have Peter, James, and John, the core triumvirate of the apostolic band, approving of violence. And they were not the only ones. One of the apostles called Simon was also nicknamed "The Zealot" (Luke 6:15). Even at this early date, zealotry stood for those who were bent on restoring Israel's independence by military force. Jesus certainly had his hands full attempting to keep his "zealous" apostles in check. And then there was Judas who evidently soured on Jesus' idea of establishing the kingdom by love and persuasion. So he rebelled and, possibly, without having thought through the ultimate consequences of his action, succeeded in handing Jesus over to the brutality of being killed by crucifixion.

We do not often think of the apostles as daring to oppose Jesus. But they did. Peter, ready to swagger a bit after having been told that his faith was the rock upon which Jesus would establish his community, made it clear that in his mind Jesus was wrong in deciding to go to Jerusalem (Mark 8:32). Suppose he were to be killed, as Jesus himself forewarned. Then there was Thomas, who remained a sceptic even after the resurrection. He, too, wanted Jesus to stay away from Jerusalem, figuring that if Jesus were killed, they would all probably be killed. "Let us go," he said resignedly to the others, "that we may die with him" (John 11:16). Of course, none of them died when Jesus was arrested because he agreed to turn himself over to his would-be captors only on condition that they let his disciples escape. And escape they did. They hid throughout the fearful ordeal of Jesus, and only those who were not members of the specially chosen apostolic band of twelve (now reduced to eleven) stayed with Jesus to the end. Among the latter were the women who had come with Jesus from Galilee and two more or less influential Jews, Nicodemus and Joseph of Arimathea, who arranged for his burial. Meanwhile, doughty Peter denied Jesus thrice during the latter's trial.

Why Leave So Poor an Image of the Apostles?

Admittedly, the apostles turn out to be a rather sorry lot in the Gospel accounts. One of the reasons is to enhance the majesty of Jesus by playing his coolness and command over against the pride and pusillanimity of the apostles. But then they are just like us. And that is the other reason for portraying them with all their faults. Jesus *puts up with* them just as God puts up with us. In the Fourth Gospel it is said that Jesus "knew all men and needed no one to bear witness of man; for he himself knew what was in man" (John 2:25; this translation, from the 1962 RSV, comes closer to the Greek text than the more recent NRSV, which tries to avoid sexist language).

Jesus knew what was in man or woman. But in the Gospels the women fare much better than the men. They are loyal; they seem to understand him and can even draw him out, like that cheeky Syrophoenician Gentile woman, and the Samaritan woman who carried on a profound theological discussion with Jesus sitting around Jacob's well (Mark 7:26; John 4:1ff.). The Gentile woman convinced Jesus that his mission was not limited to the Jews, and the Samaritan woman induced him to reveal himself earlier and more openly than he had done in Galilee. She even elicited from him the announcement that the future of religion lay neither in Samaria nor in Jerusalem, saying that in times to come people would worship in spirit and in truth, not in any particular place.

The important lesson in all the above is that God understands our weaknesses, and from a psychological and medical point of view we are just beginning to understand ourselves, our human nature, better. Some may feel that sociologists have all but done away with sin, since the way people behave is determined largely by their heredity, environment, education, health, and economic opportunities. It can hardly be denied that we now understand the influence such factors have on behavior far better than people did a century or so ago, not to mention two or three thousand years ago. The saying: "There but for the grace of God go I," recognizes how unevenly life apportions its favors. It is good to remember this when we begin to feel especially virtuous. Even decades after the resurrection, the saintliest of the apostles were behaving just like people. When Peter came up to Antioch from Jerusalem, he and Barnabas thought nothing of eating with Gentile Christians. But when emissaries from James came to Antioch from Jerusalem, Peter began again to eat apart from the Gentile Christians (Gal. 2:12). Paul then had it out with Peter and openly accused him of hypocrisy.

The crisis that arose in the relationship between Paul and Barnabas is also instructive. The two of them had taken John Mark with them on a missionary journey whose destination was Antioch in Pisidia. Arriving at Perga in Pamphylia, John Mark, whose mother had a house in Jerusalem which was a well-known rendezvous for the early followers of Jesus, decided to abandon the trip and return to mother. So, later, when Paul and Barnabas were about to set on a second missionary journey that would end in Europe, Paul refused to take John Mark along, since he had deserted them in Pamphylia. "The disagreement [between Paul and Barnabas] became so sharp that they parted company" (Acts 15:39). Barnabas took John Mark with him to Cyprus — in Acts we never hear again of either of the two — and Paul joined with Silas and pushed on to Troas and Philippi in Macedonia.

Whether Paul was right or wrong, he saw things in black and white. He was not one to compromise, a character trait which probably made him hard to get along with. But no one could accuse him of being dull or stupid. As a learned man and one who was intellectually superior to most of the apostles Jesus had originally chosen, he must have seemed to them as someone from another world. Though a Jew, he was by culture and education a Greek. He wrote and spoke Greek easily, the language of the upper class, and was well acquainted with Gentile philosophy and literature. Sometimes he must have wondered what he was doing courting the favor and approval of a group of semiliterate country fishermen.

The Human Condition

Jesus understood that it is human to err, not just make mistakes in calculation but also in moral matters. I doubt whether Peter, James, and John committed any deliberate sins while they were with Jesus. Their faults arose primarily out of ignorance. Acquiring the mentality or mind of Christ is a learning process for all of us. So we make mistakes, sometimes out of ignorance, sometimes out of weakness. People who perform actions out of sheer malice or blind hatred are to some degree insane. This does not excuse war crimes, rape, or child abuse. But when human passions are aroused, the flood gates are unbarred. Once set in motion, appetites feed on themselves and end in frenzy. At a certain point, especially where sex and violence are concerned, an individual can lose all voluntary control. We don't need well-financed studies to convince reasonably intelligent people that raw pornography and the depiction of violence stimulate the hormonal system and incline people to act out the kind of behavior they see on the screen, portrayed larger than life and in living color.

Jesus said, "You will always have the poor with you" (John 12:8). I do not limit this statement to the condition of literal penury and poverty. There is a spiritual poverty which can pervade an otherwise affluent society such as our own. Looking out over the masses of people who had come to hear him in a desert place, Jesus had compassion on them, for he saw that they were like sheep without a shepherd (Mark 6:34). He would have been stirred to a comparable compassion had he been born into almost any of the Western democracies today. The spiritually impoverished blind are being seduced by a spiritually blind leadership in the world of business, entertainment, politics. The new slavery is not the result of physical coercion but of the hidden persuaders designed by advertisers and the media to keep people in bondage to their appetites.

The trouble is that so much of what is wrong with our culture has become institutionalized. This makes it extremely hard to deal with, and it is a situation that bears a striking resemblance to organized crime, save that organized crime operates outside the law, while institutional crime is protected by the law which, in the eyes of some, makes it moral. Thus, people who work within the mega-institutions of our day may, more or less innocently, carry out the instructions handed down from above. They are loyal to the company and its objectives. They feed their families, pay their taxes, and go to church. Few reflect seriously on the fact that they are party to the very evils they so bitterly complain about.

The Games People Play

So much for society as a whole. Returning close to home, it pays to look in the mirror. Much of the distress and contention that exist in families and in business relations take place because people are not aware of the hidden wellsprings of their motivation. In his *Games People Play* Eric Berne exposes admirably not only the fact that often we not only "know not *what* we do" but, more to the point, *why* we do it.[7] Some of the names of the games Berne describes are self-explanatory, such as: See what you made me do; If it weren't for you; Ain't it awful; Yes but; I'm only trying to help, etc. After years of living or working together, people get into a rut and replay the same tapes over and over again. Whatever goes wrong, it must be somebody else's fault. Or, if one fails in some project, it is easy to fall into the habit of thinking of oneself as a born loser. Ghetto kids often repeatedly hear the message which says, "You can't make it." There are people who, if you try to help them, will reject every suggestion offered and come away victorious, having parried with a negative argument every proposal made. This is the "Yes but" syndrome. The game of "Wooden Leg" might also be called, "Poor little me." "You see, the reason why I can't cope is because I have this disability (physical, emotional, social), so don't expect me to shape up, cooperate, and do my share of the work."

An experienced psychologist or counsellor can almost immediately smoke out the games people play, though in some cases it may take a few sessions. The game playing is often carried into the consulting room, so that the client, almost unconsciously, wears a mask. He wants to assure the analyst or counsellor that there is really nothing wrong with him. In fact, the people who need counselling the most are frequently the ones most reluctant to seek help. We all need help! That is why spiritual direction is so important, even for people who are not into playing games with themselves.

I say "playing games with themselves," because before we can set out to deceive others we must first deceive ourselves. Jesus knew "what was in man." He understood how we fool ourselves, usually through ignorance. But it is an ignorance that often leads to distressing life situations for others in one's immediate surround. As Jesus said to John and James who wanted to bring fire down on the Samaritans who refused them admission to their town, "You know not the spirit that moves you" (Luke 9:55). The so-called capital sins — pride, covetousness, lust, anger, gluttony, envy, and sloth — are not really sins but only inclinations which, if acted on, can lead to sin. There is an old spiritual adage which advises: Cut things off at the root (*obsta principiis*). In other words, don't let your inclinations and appetites run away with you. We are all a bundle of energies seeking some kind of fulfillment. That is all to the good. It

---

7. New York: Grove Press, 1964.

leads to creativity. But the psychic dynamism can be destructive. So it is very important for us to get to know ourselves. To know, first of all, the nature of these fundamental human energies common to everyone; and, secondly, to recognize clearly what is peculiar to our own psychology, so that we are not driven by these inner compulsions but understand them and learn how to control them, even use them for worthy ends. They are the fuel that enables us to get up and go, to will and to accomplish. When we miscalculate or misuse these forces, we have to be patient and learn to *put up with* ourselves, without becoming discouraged or too cavalier about our shortcomings. We make mistakes in order to learn. In the end Peter learned humility. He learned to be tolerant of those who did not see things the way he did. He accepted Gentiles without prescribing what kinds of food they should eat. He apparently took Paul's rebuke well, when Paul accused him of hypocrisy. And while he himself still felt circumcision was important, he did not insist that Paul and Barnabas require Gentile converts to be circumcised.

Shrewd men and women of the world can very often spot what motivates others. They know all about the seven capital sins, though under some other name. Yet, they can be undiscerning about their own ego trips and power drives. Ignorance covers a multitude of sins. It can hide their most nasty traits from the sophisticated as well as from the masses. The longer I live the more I become convinced that the beginning of wisdom does not start with fear of the Lord but with self-knowledge. Having it himself, Jesus was able and had every right to point out to others how important it is. Were the Pharisees he criticized fully and reflexively conscious of the games they were playing with themselves and with the people? I think not. They belong to a type we shall always have with us, like ourselves, not fully aware of their own self-deception.

Knowing the blindness and limitations of people in the human condition, we should be able, with Jesus, to *put up with* the foibles of our friends, relatives, and other disagreeable people, as well as with ourselves in our seediest moments. If Jesus could tolerate the wooden-headedness of his close companions, he must surely be ready and willing to accept us, dressed as we are, warts and all, as long as we are doing the best we can. Perhaps the final word should be, as far as others are concerned: Know, but judge not. *Tout comprendre, c'est tout pardonner.*

Chapter 13

JESUS AND THE FEMININE

In spite of the great reverence in which the immediate apostles of Jesus were held in the generation during which the Gospels were being written, they appear to be anything but heroic in the actual Gospel accounts. The fact that these men are presented in a rather poor light is a credit to the evangelists. They did not idealize these men but portrayed them as self-seeking, proud, unreliable, weak-kneed, unbelieving, and, even to the end, failing to understand the substance of Jesus' teaching. When he was arrested, they fled.

Here I would like to take a brief look at the various women who make their appearance in the four Gospels. Though it may not be immediately evident, when we pay closer attention to all the Gospel accounts, it turns out that the women — almost all of them — come off with flying colors in contrast to the men. First, there is Mary, the mother of Jesus, whom the angel of the annunciation addressed as "most highly favored," and who in spite of her humility recognized that in the future "all generations would call [her] blessed." She appears a few times in Jesus' public life and in contexts that have been grossly misunderstood by many contemporary commentators. I shall treat some of these misunderstandings below. If Joseph, the father of Jesus, had died many years before Jesus became a public figure, his mother must have done most of the parenting after the father's death. A Jewish mother, in time past and even today, has usually been thought to exercise an important role in the rearing of a male child. This would be especially the case were there no father in the household. So I should not be too far from the mark were I to suggest that Jesus was influenced by his mother's outlook and set of values.

Extrapolating backward from what we know about Jesus' teaching, we would seem to be justified in assuming that Mary was a person highly sensitive to the needs of others, that she had compassion for the sick and marginalized people of her society, and that she was a deeply prayerful person. With Jesus she loved nature and the beauty of flowers, the flight of birds, and the mystery of growing things. Doing a fast forward to the later years, we find that it was Mary who launched Jesus on his ministry of teaching and miracle working. The two of them were invited, with a few of Jesus' early disciples, to a marriage feast in Cana. Toward the end of festivities, Mary called her son's attention to what was about to amount to a social disaster. "They have no wine," she said. To which Jesus replied with a question: "How does this concern you and me?" After all, Jesus was not a wine merchant who could order a cask of wine to be brought in from his cellar. Mary, who was concerned about the embarrassment of her hosts, still felt that "they" — the two of them — ought to do something. So, overriding Jesus' desire not to get involved, she turned to the servants and told them to do whatever Jesus ordered. Though in his own mind her son did not think that his "hour" for beginning his ministry had come, he nevertheless worked his first miracle at Mary's behest and changed the six jars of water into superior wine (John 2:1–11).

Some critics think that Jesus was annoyed with his mother, and instead of translating *ti emoi kai soi* as implying togetherness, "How does this concern us?" they give it a hostile sense: "Woman, what is there in common between you and me?" The sequel clearly demonstrates that this reading is fatuous; for Jesus not only does what Mary asks but it causes his disciples to believe in him and bask in his glory. It was Mary who first revealed Jesus to the world.

We have yet another instance when Jesus was reluctant to work a miracle, and once again it is a woman who prodded him into doing something he was at first reluctant to do. I am referring, of course, to that Syrophoenician woman, a Gentile, whose daughter was seriously ill with some kind of psychological disorder. She shouted after Jesus' disciples begging for a cure, but they, in an effort to protect him, tried to send her away. When the woman would not go away but kept crying aloud, Jesus, because he sincerely believed that he had no mandate to minister to the Gentiles told her that he "was not sent but to the sheep that are lost of the house of Israel" (Matt. 15:24). That would mean the Jews of the Diaspora, to which group the lady did not belong. After all, one has to feed one's own children first; then if there is anything left over, it can be fed to the servant or the dogs. Nothing daunted this persistent woman who, as a sparring partner, proved to be a match for Jesus, came back with the observation that "even the dogs eat the crumbs that fall from the master's table." Jesus was so impressed with her faith that he not only healed her daughter but he also learned a lesson. His mission was not limited to the Jews. It was for all men and women, regardless of ethnic identity, religion, or sex.

The Fourth Gospel includes a number of fairly lengthy exchanges between Jesus and someone he happens to meet, such as Nicodemus, who came to see him by night to avoid detection, or Pilate who, as a slick, sophisticated, urbane Roman, was baffled by Jesus' unworldly outlook. The longest and most profound of these encounters took place when Jesus tangled with the Samaritan woman who had all those husbands, not all at once, but successively. To begin with, Jesus did something unthinkable for a male Jewish teacher. He not only discussed a most controversial theological matter with her, a woman, but with a member of the hated Samaritan clan, a woman who was presently cohabiting with a man who was not her husband, she, having discarded five previous lovers. Returning from a shopping tour in the village, Jesus' disciples were astonished to find him talking alone with a woman of any kind, let alone a Samaritan whose past was such that she was shunned by other women. Even after she admits her unsettled past, Jesus reveals to her his true identity and confides to her that in the future people will worship in spirit and truth, not in any particular place (John 4:24).

If the Gentile woman won his admiration, Jesus was no less impressed by the faith of the woman who suffered from a flow of blood and from the ministrations of the practitioners of ancient medicine. This woman pressed through the crowd in the belief that if only she could touch Jesus, even the hem of his garment, she would be healed. And she was immediately cured of her ailment, winning from Jesus praise for her very great faith. Nor did he fail to admire the generosity of the poor widow who, in giving her small offering to the Treasury, made a sacrifice far greater than the sacrifices of those who ostentatiously gave far larger sums out of their abundance.

It seems that in Jesus' day "only women" could be guilty of sins against the sixth commandment! That was the problem of the Samaritan woman. We don't know for sure whether the woman who came in off the street to anoint the feet of Jesus with ointment and her tears of repentance was a prostitute or whether she is to be identified with Mary Magdalene out of whom Jesus cast "seven devils" (Luke 8:2). She may have been a usurer or married to a publican or a Gentile, which was considered sin enough for a Hebrew woman. In any case, Jesus called the attention of the Pharisee who was his host to the fact that her action was a symbol of her love since her sins, though many, had been forgiven. Those love most who have been forgiven most.

There is yet a fourth Mary, besides Mary the mother of Jesus, Mary Magdalene, and the "other Mary" who stood with Magdalene at the foot of the cross. She is Mary of Bethany, the sister of Martha. It was this Mary who, in the first two Synoptic Gospels, anointed the head of Jesus — not the feet in this case — with costly ointments, only to be condemned by Judas (in John's Gospel) for wasting such precious nard. However, Jesus defended her as he had defended the sinful woman, even declaring that what she had done would be celebrated "in the whole world for a memory of her" (Matt. 26:13). For Jesus sensed that this anointing had a double significance: it anticipated the anointing that would be hastily performed at the time of his burial, and it was also a kind of messianic anointing, poured now on the head rather than on the feet, as a final witness to his kingly status. That, at least, was what the evangelists seem to have had in mind, and it was a woman who paid Jesus this honor.

As suggested above, it does seem that the Gospels go out of their way to describe the compassion with which Jesus related to "fallen women," who were so often victims of poverty and male oppression. Besides the accounts of the street woman who anointed his feet and of his exchanges with the promiscuous Samaritan woman, we have the story about his defense of the woman taken in adultery. Early one morning when Jesus was sitting down in the Temple teaching the people, the scribes and Pharisees, ostentatious upholders of the letter of the Law, dragged before him a woman taken in adultery. Their idea was to test him. He was known for his kindness toward sinners, but the Law of Moses required that a woman who committed adultery should be stoned to death. Now, was Jesus going to violate the Torah and the sacred Law by letting the woman go, or would he consent to her death by stoning? Knowing men as he did, Jesus did not condemn the woman but, it would seem, challenged any man present who had not at any time had an illicit sexual affair to cast the first stone. Sheepishly, all the men withdrew from the scene, beginning with the elders, so that the woman was left alone with Jesus. Since no one remained to condemn her, neither did Jesus condemn her, but simply dismissed her with the gentle counsel not to sin again (John 8:1–11).

Why was Jesus so considerate of women accused of infidelity? Could it be that his own mother had suffered from the tongues of the malicious gossips in her village when it was discovered that she had conceived before she and Joseph had come together, and that her son had been born "prematurely"? Initially, Joseph knew nothing about the action of the Holy Spirit in Mary's virginal conception. When he first found out that she was with child, what was he to do? Thus, we read about his predicament in Matthew's Gospel: "Her husband Joseph, being a righteous man and unwilling to expose her to public disgrace, planned to dismiss her quietly" (Matt. 1:19). Had he dismissed her she still might have been subject to stoning. Yet, by not doing so, all the relatives and neighbors who could count could not fail to know that Jesus, who was a full-term baby, had been conceived before Joseph and Mary were married. Some writers have suggested that one of the reasons why Jesus received so little respect in his own village when he went to speak there was because he was regarded as illegitimate. This ties in with what Mark says in his Gospel. When Jesus sat down to teach in the synagogue at Nazareth, the congregation "took offense at him," saying, "Is this not the carpenter, the son of Mary?" (Mark 6:3). However, since Joseph seems to have died many years earlier, it may have been quite natural for the people of Nazareth to call Jesus Mary's son. On the other hand, Matthew traces the legal ancestry of Jesus through Joseph and twice refers to him as "the son of Joseph" (John 1:45; 6:42). Luke says he was only "thought" to be Joseph's son (Luke 3:23).

His Women Friends

In any case, Jesus treated women with great respect. He had many women friends and he seemed to be completely at ease in their presence, whether they were young or old. Luke mentions by name a number of women who travelled about with Jesus and his disciples: Magdalene, Joanna, a certain Susanna, "and many others" (Luke 8:3). Among the "others" must have been Martha, who on one occasion had received Jesus into her home. Both she and her sister Mary were devoted to Jesus, though quite different in temperament from one another, as we learn from Luke. It is he who tells the story about the busy Martha and the contemplative Mary. Martha was concerned with preparing earthly food, while Mary fed on the teaching of Jesus. Jesus himself was acquainted with this spiritual food. When the disciples returned from the Samaritan village where they had gone to buy food, they asked Jesus to "eat something." But he said to them, "I have a food to eat that you do not know about" (John 4:32).

Martha and Mary also turn up in John's Gospel at the time when their brother Lazarus had died. Martha, always a dynamo of action, goes out to meet Jesus the moment she hears that he is near. She chides him for having delayed an extra day before coming to Lazarus's side. "Lord," she complains, "if you had been here, my brother would not have died." But, she adds trustingly "I know that he will rise again on the last day." This remark elicits from Jesus the declaration that has

echoed down the ages: "I am the resurrection and the life; he who believes in me, though he die, yet shall he live" (John 11:25). In reply,
Martha, a woman, makes the confession in John's Gospel that was assigned to Peter in the Synoptics: "You are the Christ, the Son of God"
(Matt. 16:16; John 11:27).

The Woman

What is noticeable in John's Gospel, and to an equal extent in Luke's,
is the important role assigned to women. If the birth of Jesus is told
from the point of view of Joseph, a man, in Matthew's Gospel, Mary is
featured in Luke's. If Joseph never utters a word, Mary not only speaks
but meditates, taking to heart all the events she has been party to (Luke
2:51). Elizabeth and the prophetess Anna both have an important role
to play in relation to Mary.

John features Mary at the beginning and conclusion of Jesus' public ministry. She stretches from Cana to Calvary and beyond. Mary is
not the only woman to follow Jesus to Calvary. The other Galilean
women "stood at a distance and saw these things," while the apostles
were prominently absent. But John situates Mary, at least in spirit, at
the foot of the cross. And he does this with a definite purpose in mind.
Through Mary, and in the person of the Beloved Disciple, he will show
that those who believe in Christ are his sisters and brothers, spiritual
children of the same mother.

Above all, Mary is "The Woman" *(Hē Gunē)*. Jesus called her by that
name at Cana, when he said, "Woman, how does this [shortage of wine]
concern us?" (John 2:4). Now, on Calvary, speaking from the cross,
he once again addresses Mary as "Woman." Referring to the Beloved
Disciple, who is standing with Mary beneath the cross, Jesus says to
her, "Woman, here is your son." He then addresses the Disciple and
says, regarding Mary, "Here is your mother." Note that Jesus calls Mary
both mother and woman. The Beloved Disciple stands for all those who
believe in Christ. They are Jesus' brothers and sisters because they have
the same spiritual mother, that is, Mary. The Beloved Disciple, now her
"other son," is a stand-in for all Mary's children. Like Eve, the Woman,
Mary is the "Mother of all the living" (Gen. 3:20). The Fathers of the
Church have consistently regarded Mary as the Second Eve, alongside
Jesus, the Second Adam. In any case, she appears as the consort of Jesus
in his universal ministry, lest the Incarnation be viewed as a strictly male
affair. Simeon had said of Mary at the time of Jesus' presentation in

the Temple, "A sword will pierce your own soul, too" (Luke 2:35). If St. Paul can say, I am "co-crucified" with Christ (*synestaurōmai*), how much more deeply must Mary have identified with and been co-crucified with her son? (Gal. 2:19). Her fidelity and presence beneath the Tree of the Cross reverses Eve's infidelity beneath the Tree of the Knowledge of Good and Evil in the Garden of Eden. Mary, for the author of the Fourth Gospel, is the Everlasting Woman.

In Revelation she is presented as "a great portent in heaven: a woman clothed with the sun, with the moon under her feet, and on her head a crown of twelve stars" (Rev. 12:1). The Woman *(Hē Gunē)* of Revelation is both the church persecuted by the forces of evil and the mother of Jesus, she who "gave birth to a son, a male child who is to rule all the nations with a rod of iron" (Rev. 12:5). The author of the final book of the Christian Bible seems to have had two things in mind: first, identifying the mother of the male child with the woman clothed with the sun, while also presenting Mary as the icon symbolizing or personifying the church as the mother of those living with divine life. She is *Theotokos,* the God-bearer; *Christo-pher*, the Christ-bearer; or *Luci-fer*, the Light-bearer, the Morning Star, preceding yet radiant with the rising sun's light. Revelation, like the Fourth Gospel, is telling us something about the mystery of Mary as the consort of Jesus in bringing life to the world. She is a symbol of the archetypal feminine on the spiritual plane, and her relevance has been carefully underlined by both John and Luke.

In the Gospels, the women are not only the first to witness the resurrection of Jesus but, unlike the apostles who were still in hiding, they were able to testify to the events surrounding the crucifixion of Jesus. This is contrary to the position of some scripture scholars who hold that the evangelists had no way of knowing what took place on Calvary beyond the fact of Jesus' crucifixion, since not one of the apostles was there. The Gospels are unanimous in saying that the women were there. They also came on the first day of the week to complete the anointing of Jesus' body in the tomb. There is no record of the apostles rising early, once the Sabbath was over, and coming to the tomb in a courageous display of respect and devotion. Consequently, it was not the men who first witnessed the resurrection but the women. It must have been hard for the evangelists to admit that the women took precedence over the men, an admission so against the grain that it can hardly be an invention of the Gospel writers.

Surely one of the most touching episodes in John's Gospel is Magdalene's mistaking the risen Jesus for some kind of early morning gardener. She found the tomb empty and fearing that someone had taken the body of Jesus away and hidden it somewhere, she offers to go and get it, "and I will take him away" (John 20:15). How she was supposed to manage this operation was not thought out by Magdalene, but love knows no obstacle. When the risen Jesus finally calls her by her name, she recognizes the voice and turns to cling to him. Like the Shulammite in the Song of Solomon, Magdalene wants to exclaim: "I have found him whom my soul loves. I held him and would not let him go" (Song 3:4). But Jesus has work for her to do. She is to go and announce the resurrection to the men and tell them that he will soon be departing from them, since he will be ascending into heaven to their common Father (John 20:17).

Thus, even before any of the apostles had seen the risen Christ or even believed in his victory over death, Jesus showed his tender concern for his loyal women followers by appearing to them first, before he manifested his presence to Peter or James or any of the other male disciples.

Paul

The place of women in the culture Jesus was born into was extremely restrictive. A man could easily divorce a woman and put her away simply by writing a bill of divorce. Women had no such right. The woman taken in adultery in John's Gospel was threatened with stoning, but there is no indication that her illicit lover was under a similar threat. Yet, according to the Book of Leviticus (20:10), "If a man commits adultery with the wife of his neighbor, both the adulterer and the adulteress shall be put to death." In practice, the male offender was rarely punished.

People in the women's movement have every right to be shocked by the kind of misogyny assigned to Paul in the New Testament. In his defense it must be said that the First Letter to Timothy ascribed to Paul is almost certainly a pseudonymous composition, dating from the end of the first century years after Paul's death. In the Letter to Timothy, the author rules: "Let women learn in silence in all submissiveness. I permit no women to teach or have authority over men; she is to keep silent." Why? "Because Adam was formed first, then Eve; and Adam was not deceived, but the woman was deceived and became a transgressor" (1 Tim. 2:12–14). One thing is clear. When the letter was composed, women must have been exercising authority over men, talking and preaching in church, and perhaps even officiating at the Eucharist. Otherwise, why would the author of the letter rail so fiercely against practices that did not exist? Again, in defense of Paul, it should also be mentioned that the editors of the NRSV of the New Testament add in a footnote to 1 Corinthians 14:33–36 that some scholars "take these culturally conditioned verses as editorial insertions." The questionable text reads: "Women should be silent in the churches. For they are not permitted to speak, but should be subordinate, as the law also says. If there is anything they desire to know, let them ask their husbands at home. For it is shameful for a woman to speak in church." The similarity between this text and the one from 1 Timothy leads one to suspect that the idea in Timothy has been retrojected back into 1 Corinthians.

Valerie Abrahamsen holds that "in pre-Pauline and Pauline Christian communities, women appear to have functioned almost identically to men. In fact, it is possible that more women than men were house-church leaders."[8] So while we might be able to exonerate Paul, there was enough anti-feminism in the later church to induce some writers to insert demeaning references to women in the scriptures.

Since a woman's long hair "is her glory" and possibly an occasion for vanity and a distraction for men, Paul did not want women to parade their ornate coiffures in church, admitting that his preference is only a matter of custom. And far from forbidding a woman to speak in church, he only asks that they — and presumably the men, too — cover their heads when they speak out in prophecy. This statement in 1 Corinthians 11:5 contradicts the dubious passage in 14:34 which forbids women to speak in church under any circumstances. In any case, neither men nor women are independent of one another, and both are subject to God (1 Cor. 11:11).

So while the authentic Paul insists on the equality of the sexes "in the Lord" (11:11), this was far from the case toward the end of the first century, when ecclesiastical authority was vested in men and some of the scriptures were designed to reduce women to a subservient role.

How different was the attitude of Jesus. He was always ready to learn from a woman: from his mother, from a Gentile woman, or from a poor widow woman. He confided some of his most important revelations to women. He never treated them as in any way inferior to men even when they were thought of as sinners. While other teachers in Israel kept a safe distance from women — and lepers — Jesus allowed the most despised among women to touch him and kiss his feet. If he had any objection to having a woman speak in a synagogue, he never voiced it, nor was he

---

8. "Women in the Early Christian Movement," *The Companion to the Oxford Bible* (New York: Oxford University Press), 816.

preoccupied with whether or not women covered their hair, since he allowed a woman of dubious virtue to use her flowing hair to dry the tears she had shed on his feet. Unlike almost all his male contemporaries, he did not regard a wife as the property of her husband. When a Sadducee asked him about whose wife a woman who had been married several times would be in the resurrection, since she had been "had as wife" by all seven husbands, Jesus replied that she would not be "had" by any of the men as a possession, as though she were chattel, because in the world to come they neither give nor receive in marriage, "but are like the angels of heaven" (Mark 12:25).

Would Jesus have ordained a woman? Perhaps a better question is whether he ever ordained men. It is true that the presbyterate and episcopate grew up very early in the infant church and rapidly became institutionalized. But when at the Last Supper Jesus asked those present to remember him and "do this" in the days to come, that is, break bread and partake of wine in his memory, he put no restrictions on this request by limiting it to those present, to born Jews or Gentile converts, to young or old, slave or free, male or female.

Few casual Christians realize how radical Jesus was in his social thinking. They may have some vague notion that he was opposed to religious formalism and hypocrisy, that he cured on the Sabbath and even allowed his apostles to eat with unwashed hands, or that he was not unduly concerned about what kind of food he ate. But, in fact, his social reforms called for the dismantling of the entire temple of religious prejudices and presumptions until not a stone would be left on a stone that was not thrown down (Mark 13:2). Among his all but unprecedented innovations for his part of the world was his respect for and attitude toward women. Because of the limits imposed on him by the culture of his day, there were reforms he could not immediately initiate without alienating the vast majority of his contemporaries, with the result that they would not even stay to hear his message. But he planted the seeds for future understanding and development. If one traces out the logic of his relationship with women, it would eventually entail guaranteeing their social, political, and religious equality in relation to their male counterparts. This would necessarily involve the right and duty of women to participate fully with men in the chief deliberative, legislative, and executive branches of the various Christian communities, especially in those areas that are the special concerns of women, concerns which women, not men, should be allowed to implement and legislate for.

In a country in which women are increasingly prominent in the legal and medical professions, in which the two most important offices in the president's cabinet, that of attorney general and secretary of state, are held by women, and in which state governors and United States senators are women, there is something curiously archaic about ecclesiastical gatherings, conferences, and Ecumenical Councils in which all authority and decision making is restricted to males, in some cases celibate males. But ingrained habits of mind and emotions are hard to alter or eradicate, so it would be rash to assume that the attitude toward women in the more conservative churches is likely to match that of Jesus or change abruptly. Still, as the evolution of religious consciousness continues, the direction it is taking does suggest that somewhere down the line the full dignity, equality, and capability of women will be recognized and accepted in practice as well as in theory. Never say never.

"With *men* this may be impossible, but with God all things are possible" (Matt. 19:26).

Chapter 14

THE CROSS OF JESUS AND
THE MYSTERY OF HIS BEING

Apollinaris, bishop of Laodicea, held the later condemned doctrine that, although the body and vital soul of the man Jesus were created, the intellectual principle that governed his understanding was divine. Therefore, on the rational level, Christ was omniscient, since on the level of knowing he was divine. The Jesus of the Fourth Gospel does come close to being omniscient. The Synoptic Jesus, on the other hand, grew in wisdom as he matured to full manhood (Luke 2:52). If he were omniscient, would he have deliberately chosen Judas as an apostle? Would he, as a youth, have tarried three days in the Jerusalem Temple asking questions of the leading teachers of the day in order to learn from them? In Mark's Gospel, he acknowledged that he had no certain knowledge about the Last Day (Mark 13:32). There are instances when he appears to lack any advanced knowledge about medical matters and seems to have equated emotional and organic disorders with demonic infestation. Raymond E. Brown says that Jesus — or more probably the evangelist — attributed to Abiathar the role assigned to his father Ahimelech (2 Sam. 21:2–7; Mark 2:26).

While the evangelists do not like to set limits to Jesus' human knowledge and powers, they never deny his full humanity. As pointed out in chapter 10, the Letter to the Hebrews declares that it was through suffering that he learned the cost of obedience (Heb. 5:8). Quite independent of scripture, it should be fairly evident that if Jesus was to function in any way as a model to be imitated by others, he would have to be someone who shared in those things that are common to humanity. Among such characteristics are the ability to learn, the need for food, drink, sleep, and subjection to the typically human experiences of joy, sorrow, and disappointment. That Jesus could suffer mentally, emotionally, and physically is evident from the accounts of his passion.

How much did the young Jesus know about his nature and destiny? Did he ever at any time think seriously about himself as the promised

Messiah, say, at the age of ten? Some may recall having been assured in Sunday School or catechism class that Jesus hanging on the cross knew everyone's future secret thoughts, words, and actions because, after all, he was God. Pious exaggeration trivializes the work of Jesus by denying that he truly shared our humanity. Even with regard to sin, the Synoptic Gospels say that he was tempted or tested, and while they discretely avoid any suggestion that he was troubled by carnal temptations, it would be reassuring to believers to know that Jesus was a normal human being.

Origin and Family

Reading about Jesus' preaching and miracles, one is apt to forget that he was a member of a human family and that his relations with his kinfolk were anything but smooth. The Synoptics refer to four brothers and an undisclosed number of sisters as Jesus' siblings (Mark 6:3). Jewish families tended to be large and an extended family, including cousins, might run to forty or fifty people. Village life was a tightknit affair with everyone knowing everyone else's business. I am not interested here in determining whether the family relatives of Jesus were stepbrothers and stepsisters, but only wish to point out that all four Gospels indicate that the family of Jesus, specifically his brothers, did not think very highly of him, possibly out of jealousy because of his growing renown or, as the saying goes, "prophets are not without honor except in their own country and in their own house" (Matt. 13:58). Luke (4:29) says that Jesus was physically assaulted and driven out of his own hometown, and the Fourth Gospel adds that "not even his own brothers believed in him" (John 7:5).

Who Is My Father?

In the folktales of different nations, one of the blessings a young man seeks is his father's approval. Only when he has lived up to the expectations and high standards his father has set for him will the father acknowledge the young man as his beloved son in whom he is well pleased. The quest for the father's approval is built into the story of Jesus. From his youth, as Luke's Gospel informs us, Jesus was deeply concerned with the sense in which God was his father. Without necessarily rejecting his human parentage, he told Joseph and Mary, when they found him in the Temple at the age of twelve listening to the rabbis and asking them questions, that he was only busying himself with the concerns of his Father in heaven (Luke 2:49).

In the early years it may have been largely a one-sided affair. Jesus might think of God as Father, but did the Father regard him as a true son? Usually when a man or woman has a great spiritual breakthrough, it comes as an answer to a question that had been uppermost in his or her mind: Is there a God? Why is there evil in the world? Does God love and approve of me?

The Synoptic Gospels tell us that in a personal apocalypse the heavens opened for Jesus, and a voice was heard declaring, "You are my Son, the Beloved, with you I am well pleased" (Mark 1:11). To which the Voice might have added, "Now, does that answer your question?" The breakthrough was sufficiently powerful to drive Jesus out into the desert where he could meditate on the significance of what had happened to him for the traditional forty days. (The Jews wandered in the desert for forty years and Jesus appeared to his disciples for a period of forty days after his resurrection. "Forty" means a fairly long time.)

Having had one nagging question answered, Jesus, alone in the wilderness, was now faced with a second one. If he was God's Son in some special way, what did this imply? Was he the Messiah? If so, he could probably work miracles, defy gravity, rule the world. These musings are presented in the Gospels of Matthew and Luke as temptations of the devil. Whatever their origin, they are the kind of thoughts one might expect would occur to a man convinced of God's unconditional love and favor. What Jesus learned in the desert was not that he was the Messiah, but that all men and women were God's beloved children, and that his task was to work tirelessly for the spiritual and social welfare of others. The program he developed in those weeks of isolation and prayer is outlined in the Sermon on the Mount and in the material found in the discourse at the Last Supper in John's Gospel.

The Mystery of Christ

In some of what follows I am indebted to Yves Raguin's monograph "Le Christ et son mystère," which I found hauntingly suggestive.[9]

Theologians and mystical writers, such as Meister Eckhart, have held that it often happens that, without any explicit awareness, gifted souls

---

9. *Vie Chrétienne*, Supplément, November 1979, 1–64.

do at times have a sense of their true origin and being in God. What remains hidden from us most of the time would, in Jesus' case, have become the subject of a growing awareness that began at a very early age. In the Gospels this awareness is communicated in anthropomorphic and personalist terms, as Jesus speaks of God as Father, on the analogy of human fatherhood. And Paul speaks of human fatherhood as patterned on the Fatherhood of God. It might be more accurate to think of the Fatherhood of God as patterned after our human understanding of what fatherhood means. But all such analogies break down when we try to talk about the ineffable nature of God. The absolute transcendence of God as "I Am" lies, ultimately, beyond male or female, father or mother categories. The Almighty cannot be categorized or situated within a genus or species. Judaism was well aware of this and for that reason has always refused to "name" God. For naming means knowing and having power over that which is named.

God is beyond all knowing in the subject-object sense. That is why even the spark of divinity that is latent in each one of us as images of God lies beyond all direct knowing. At privileged moments it is possible to become aware of the pure subject that one is. But we cannot have reflexive consciousness of it. It cannot be "seen," even conceptually.

I have gradually come to believe that Jesus was able fully to understand the mystery of his own being only toward the end of his life, perhaps only at the moment of his death on the cross. All along, he could not fail to know that he was different from the people around him, that somewhere in the deepest regions of his soul he seemed to remember a glory he had before coming into the world. But coming into the world and assuming a body resulted in obscuring the clear vision of his true nature. He was periodically assured of that nature on several occasions when he had peak experiences in the realm of the spirit, for example, at the time of his baptism or when on Mt. Tabor he was reassured of his favor with God. Even the healings he was party to and his command over nature communicated to him a sense of his intense union with God.

People who believe in reincarnation maintain that it is not surprising that we fail to remember our past incarnate lives, since we cannot even remember the first year or two of our lives in the present body. The self that reincarnates, they say, retains traces of past lives which at times can be reactivated at privileged moments or in regressive therapy. I prefer a modified version of Plato's myth of reminiscence. He calls it "a likely story" or "verisimilitude." It is a mythic way of talking about a very mysterious human ability. It concerns the way in which we recognize and respond to values such as justice, truth, or goodness without ever having been taught to do so. But we could not recognize such values unless we already knew them on some higher, universal level. Plato, who believed in the preexistence of the human soul, said in his myth, that before entering the body each human soul was given a glimpse of absolute Truth and Goodness. This vision was imprinted on the soul. And now when we experience instances of goodness or beauty or truth, we recognize them as being something we already know.

If Jesus came into the world as an unqualified "I am," this was something he gradually came to remember, recognize, and understand. His daily remembrance of divine approval, his holiness, and his healing powers would all converge to make the mystery of his being more accessible to him. Remembering became knowing, and knowing terminated in seeing; so that he could eventually say that he only did the things he saw the Father doing. He became like a shadow obeying in every movement the movements of the hand that cast it.

When we first meet Jesus as he begins his public life after his baptism, he is already on the way to knowing who he is. He remembers. If this sounds less attractive than the rather common misunderstanding to the effect that Jesus, even as an infant, knew all there is to know and was fully aware that he was divine, a more modest and plausible view may help some disaffected people recover a deeper sense of his humanity. There is a species of Gnosticism that would regard the humanity of Jesus as an illusion and deny that there could be any development in Jesus' understanding of his own nature because, after all, he was God. Put that way, it deprives him of a believable human nature with the associated consequence that it would be quite impossible for anyone to "follow him," since he was not truly imitable but of a species different from ours.

When Jesus, after his baptism and forty-day retreat in the desert came into Galilee, "proclaiming the good news of God, and saying, 'The time is fulfilled, and the kingdom of God has come near'" (Mark 1:14–15), he was not thinking of his betrayal, arrest, and crucifixion. He led his life "humanly," deliberating on what he should do next, eagerly giving himself and his services to the people. It was only toward the midpoint of his mission that he began to see in dim outline how it would all turn out. It was then that he began to say that the things concerning him were coming to an end, not in detail but in a general way, since he foresaw that his enemies would finally succeed in killing him. Similarly, because of the highly turbulent political climate of the times, he could also foresee that the Zealots, the Sicarii, and the Assassins in their foolish ambition to challenge Rome were all but inviting the destruction of the nation.

Whether Jesus read the scriptures and applied them to himself as his followers would do later on is hard to determine. If, in his more reflective and prayerful moments, he gave thought to the belief of some that he was the Messiah or at least, with the Baptist, the herald of the Messianic Age, no scripture declared that the Messiah would be God Incarnate, an idea so repugnant to a pious Jew that the very thought would have been equivalent to blasphemy. So, if Jesus began to experience a God-consciousness that was in open violation of the most binding restrictions of his own faith and culture, in the beginning it must have caused him a great deal of anxiety. Was there something wrong with him? Was he mad? Self-deluded? Demon-possessed? A blasphemer and therefore a sinner? We do not normally think of Jesus suffering distress over such personal uncertainties. Could he ever have been in doubt, perplexed? Take your choice: The Jesus of the Fourth Gospel who was in total control of every aspect of his life, who never had to make any decisions when in doubt, because he was possessed of a humanity that was so united with divinity that it shared in the divine omniscience; or, a Jesus who looked to God for guidance, who was often unsure of what his next move should be, and who spent the nights in prayer seeking to discern God's will for him.

Christians of most denominations are brought up with the assurance that Jesus was, if not Superman, something like Olympian Athena who sprang full-panoplied from the brow of Zeus. He had nothing to learn since a divine person could not advance from not knowing, or ignorance, to the acquisition of knowledge. Learning that Jesus was endowed with gifts of this kind would not be especially helpful for those seeking to follow him. No, from the point of view of human experience, Jesus came only gradually to discern the mystery of his being.

Know Thyself

To the extent that there is "that of God" in each one of us, we have access to the mystery of Jesus. We cannot even begin to understand his mystery until we have made some progress in understanding the mystery of our own being. Reading scripture or the lives of the saints, meditating, listening to sermons, meeting self-realized persons can help. But we do not meet the divine in ourselves by concentrating on what is external.

The best that objective studies and encounters can do is stimulate us to make progress in our own self-discovery.

St. Augustine, who was familiar with the Greek adage "Know thyself," held that the path to divine knowledge was through the soul, that is, one must begin with self-knowledge. Because the soul is the image of God, the better one knows the soul, the better will be one's chance of knowing and loving God. The same is true of our knowledge of Jesus. True self-knowledge helps one appreciate his interior life. Light on him casts further light on our own being. Then as we deepen our self-awareness, we penetrate more deeply into Jesus' experience of his own mystery.

The Faith of Jesus

To enter this loop of coexistence with Jesus, faith is needed. It is not the product of convoluted rational analysis, nor will sheer willfulness enable anyone to enter the kingdom. The kind of faith Jesus had was not based on deductive or inductive reason, neither did it consist in a blind acceptance of a set of doctrinal propositions. It was an orientation of the heart, suffused with loving trust in the wisdom and goodness of God, come what may.

Just as Jesus increased in wisdom, maturity, and grace, so those who follow him are to retrace a similar program of awareness. St. Paul did not think the parallel between our experience and the experience of Jesus was unfounded. The goal of the spiritual life is to attain "the measure of the full stature of Christ" (Eph. 4:13). In the Letter to the Hebrews, Jesus is called the "pioneer and perfecter of our faith" (Heb. 12:2). He is the model for our own faith and trust in God. It is surely another grave misunderstanding to suppose that Jesus had no need of faith because, even in his humanity, he enjoyed the full and unmediated vision of God at all times. If he was to share fully in our humanity with all its limitations, sin alone excluded, then he, too, must have had to live by faith.

Great must have been the faith and trust of Jesus in facing death — and such a death as he endured — while being convinced that he would overcome what some call the last great enemy. The resurrection spells out the measure of his faith, a faith stronger than death. The lesson should not be lost on those who die, a fate which, so far, no flesh has managed to escape but only postpone. Faith and human effort go hand in hand. And once it is understood that one cannot overcome human weakness and vulnerability by sheer will power, the way is open for faith, whose gropings probe beyond what deductive reasoning and mere tenacity can achieve.

What filled the gap between what Jesus knew as a normal and intelligent human being and his ultimate victory over death was not the kind of faith that illumines the intelligence on the details of how to act in a given situation, nor does it tell one what to do next in everyday life. That is why Jesus had to deliberate prayerfully before choosing a path, in selecting his disciples, in deciding where to preach next, when to go to Jerusalem, how to answer his adversaries.

This is not to say that Jesus did not enjoy intimations, often very insistent ones, by which to guide his life. But for the most part he had only a generic kind of faith to live by, confident that if he were to go to the cross his trust would be vindicated in the end. The author of the Fourth Gospel was intuitively right when he represented Jesus as scanning the horizon of his spirit to discover and respond to what he called his Father's will. The big picture was clear to him. Only gradually were the painful details unveiled. The same is true of all who seek to be led by the Spirit. John Henry Newman summed it up in his prayer: "Lead, Kindly Light, amidst the encircling gloom.... One step enough for me."

Concerning the Future

Did Jesus know the future? For example, did he know that he would be regarded as the founder of a world religion that would number hundreds of millions of souls among its members? Did he know that he would be proclaimed the unique and indispensable savior of the entire human race? I seriously doubt that his conjectural knowledge included a clear and detailed vision of the future. On the other hand, contrary to what some commentators hold, I do not doubt that, after his experience on Mt. Tabor when he was transfigured in glory, he knew in his heart that he would be killed. Luke says that some friendly Pharisees warned Jesus that Herod Antipas, who ruled Galilee, wanted to kill him. The Jewish historian Josephus says that Herod, seeing how John the Baptist was gathering large crowds around him, and fearing he might use his influence to stir up a rebellion, "thought it best, by putting him to death, to prevent any mischief he might cause."[10] So Jesus had every reason to

---

10. *The Antiquities of the Jews*, 18, 5, 2.

fear Herod. Mark writes that he warned his disciples on at least three
occasions (Mark is fond of threes) that he would be killed (Mark 8:31;
9:31; 10:33–34). The predictions became increasingly more detailed as
Jesus could see which way the wind was blowing. In the earliest prediction, he says that he will be rejected by the Jewish leadership, the elders,
the high priests, and the scribes, and killed, presumably by stoning, as
would happen in the case of Stephen later on. The second prediction includes the notion of "betrayal," which suggests that at some point along
the way Jesus began to sense the disaffection of Judas. Finally, Jesus lets
it be known that those who are out to kill him are not just the Temple
authorities but the Romans too. That is a far more alarming prospect;
for the Romans not only crucified men condemned to death but very
often nearly scourged them to death before hanging them on a tree. Unlike the Jewish custom for penal scourging, Roman scourging was not
limited to thirty-nine strokes. So if Jesus was turned over to the Romans, he could expect to be severely scourged with leather thongs and
leaded balls before his execution. And, in fact, so severe was the scourging Jesus received that he was unable to carry his own cross. The soldiers
had to commandeer Simon of Cyrene, a man from the crowd, to carry
the crossbeam to the hill of Calvary.

I mention Jesus' foretelling his own death and, eventually, the kind of
death he would undergo, to counter the charge, for example of Rudolf
Bultmann, to the effect that all the passages where Jesus foretells his
death and the circumstances connected with it are prophecy by hindsight
(*vaticinia ex eventu*), introduced by the evangelists to stress Jesus' divine
foreknowledge. No; since he did live in dangerous times, and since he
was on the wanted list of both Pilate and the Temple priesthood (who
lived hand in glove with their Roman overlords), it required no great
stretch of the imagination for Jesus to have foreseen what his fate would
be and who would probably be responsible for it.

And so it turned out. Going to Jerusalem, Jesus escaped the clutches
of Herod only to be betrayed in Judea by a close disciple. Was it all
planned? Jesus went to extraordinary lengths to make sure Judas did
not know beforehand where the Last Supper was to be held. He had no
doubt already been informed by friends connected with the Sanhedrin,
such as Joseph of Arimathea or Nicodemus, that Judas was in the process of making a deal with the Jewish authorities. So it was important
that he celebrate what might very well be his last meal without interrup-
tion. Knowing, earlier on, what was in store for him — I am speculating
here — I think that Jesus in a sense threw caution to the wind and
decided, as one of his final acts, to cleanse the Temple by driving out

the money-changers. I think he also carefully planned his so-called "triumphal entry" into Jerusalem on Palm Sunday as a kind of formal and official act of bringing his message to the nation's citadel. During the following days, according to Matthew's Gospel, he preached and taught in the Temple area, offering many parables, answering questions, and denouncing the scribes and Pharisees. It was a kind of public swan song.

The fact that Jesus was hailed by the crowd on Palm Sunday as Son of David, that is, as king and heir to the throne of David, was enough to convince the Romans that things had gone too far. He had to be stopped. Then his attack on the Temple, coupled with his prediction that it would be destroyed, must have counted heavily against him during his Jewish trial. Since the Temple was the dwelling place of God, any kind of attack on it, even a verbal one, would have been regarded as an attack on God. One cannot exaggerate the horror even a suggestion of the Temple's destruction would have provoked in the minds of pious Jews, let alone the high priests whose very living depended on the Temple's survival. So when the high priest accused Jesus of blasphemy (Matt. 26:65), it was not entirely beside the point, at least from his angle of vision.

The Meaning of the Cross

As we move now to a consideration of the passion and death of Jesus, we have the prime example of his acting out his own teaching. Following the interior light that brought him to Jerusalem in the first place, he showed that he was indeed willing to lose his life in order to find it. His death and resurrection symbolize this teaching.

How could one who taught a doctrine as sublime as that attributed to Jesus, and who lived it out so completely himself, end his life on what is probably the most infamous instrument of torture ever invented by the perverted human mind? The cross had to be a stumbling block or scandal to the Jews of his day and pure foolishness to the Gentiles (1 Cor. 1:23). Do we not have here a case of *perfect* injustice? As I said earlier, maybe one of the revelations the death of Jesus is meant to unveil is that there is no correlation between virtue and good fortune. The good often die young, the unjust prosper, the innocent are victimized. That is the way of the world. It is easy to profess allegiance to God when fortune smiles, but once let tragedy strike and those whose faith is fragile will quickly lose hope and desert ship.

Trust in God should not depend on whether or not things are going well for us. Most people can sustain a modicum of adversity, but in the lives of some there comes a time when it feels as though God has either abandoned them or does not exist. The cry of Jesus from the cross, "My God, my God, why have you forsaken me!" recorded in the Gospel according to Mark and repeated in Matthew, has been interpreted in a variety of ways. For some it might seem that Jesus had despaired. Others say that he was simply repeating on his own behalf the psalm traditionally used by Jews for the dying. Or the evangelists may have introduced the Psalm 22 because they saw in it a preview of what was actually taking place on Calvary: Jesus was being mocked by his enemies, his bones were out of joint, his hands and feet were pierced, and the soldiers were casting lots for his garments.

But there is another mystical interpretation which might come closer to the mystery of Jesus and his own experience. Since childhood he had always looked to the Father for guidance. It was this vision of the Father that he consulted when he needed to receive light on how he should act. But on the cross the vision of the Father as an object outside himself had forsaken him. Stripped of every conceivable human possession and sign of dignity, abandoned by his friends, rejected by the leaders of his own nation, stretched on a deathbed that was not his own, buried in another man's tomb, there was nothing left for Jesus in the realm of having. Only the naked "I am" and his vision of the Father remained. Then unaccountably that vision was eclipsed, and it left him at the very moment when he needed it most. Through all the years the Father had always stood before him and accompanied him everywhere, like the Shekinah or symbol of the divine presence that accompanied the people of Israel day and night as they wandered in the wilderness for forty years. Now even that was gone.

In Philippians Paul speaks of the self-emptying of Jesus, his pouring out (*exinanitio, kenosis*) or self-divestiture. Here on the cross with open arms, with nothing to hide, in the nothingness of all that was still human, all that remained was the naked Self, the Nothingness of the One Who Is, the "I am" without a second, beyond all naming and qualifying attributes. Having abandoned family, fortune, and every semblance of pride and power, was it not fitting that the one who came to serve the powerless, marginalized people of the earth should be like the least of them in death, so as to become in the eyes of the proud a nonperson, a nobody?

If Jesus has earned any title to divinity, one should not omit from consideration an outpouring so total that nothing was left of the merely human. In the naughting of the human, all that remained was the burning flame of divinity. It was the moment when the divinity absorbed all that was left of his humanity to preserve it and unite it forever to his Person in the transcendent order. It was the moment when Jesus had the nondual experience, when he could say, "I and the Father are one.... Whoever sees me sees the Father." His humanity had become so completely taken up into the divinity, that the Father was no longer an object, related as subject to object, but as subject in subject.

Some people see the death of Jesus as a painful payback to God for human wickedness. I prefer to see it as a model for all who suffer physical, moral, or emotional distress, along with persecution for right-eousness' sake. God may seem to be most absent when we are in pain, but with the starvation of every access to pleasure, in the unwanted thwarting of the will, in the mortification or dying which life eventually imposes on all of us, there often stirs in the deeper reaches of the soul another kind of life. It will come to the surface in those who die gracefully by accepting their mortality and even welcoming it as a stage of growth. When this has been achieved, one has already risen from the dead, even as Jesus did at the moment of his death on the cross.

Part Three

ETERNAL LIFE

Chapter 15

GOD'S OFFSPRING

Western Christianity has been characteristically shy about celebrating the full meaning of the Gospel teaching that we are "born of God" and "children of God." We hear the expression so often that we have almost forgotten the full force of the first two words of the Lord's Prayer, "Our Father." The teaching that we are made in the image of God or that we are partakers in the divine nature has been reduced to an almost meaningless formula. Yet, the divinity of the believer is an open secret. It is written all over the New Testament. But were a preacher to declare the divinity of those in his or her congregation, many would think that the minister was teaching heresy!

There is a definite inclination to trivialize the revelation of our true status as children of God. We are apt to think of it as a mere metaphor or, in trying to avoid speaking of both men and women as "sons" of God in order to avoid sexist language, we employ the neutral word "children." But adult human beings are not children. St. Paul avoids the implication of immaturity when he declares that "we are indeed God's offspring" (Acts 17:28). Since he is in Athens on the Areopagus talking to pagan Greeks, he does not intend to limit participation in the divine life to Jews or baptized Christians. Elsewhere, he says that those who have received the spirit of sonship are entitled to address God as Jesus did when he addressed the Lord as "Abba! Father!" (Rom. 8:15).

The important thing is not to debate whether or not we are God's offspring and, therefore, participants in the divine life, but to understand that this participation is not the same as *realizing* our kinship with God. Whether we are consciously aware of it or not, we are made in the image of God. This is true of a man, a woman, or an unborn fetus. You cannot *become* an image of God or, on the occasion of baptism, suddenly *become* divine. The divine image can neither be lost nor acquired.

What follows must of its very nature be speculative. For I will argue that all human beings, whether Christian or not, are in the image of God, and that this includes having a share in divinity. What, then, does the image entail beyond intelligence and freedom? I think one must add immortality. It is hard to see how that which exists as the image of God could be essentially perishable, to which statement I would add that I do not think that the immortality of the image is a miracle, but that it is something intrinsic to it as image. One should not confuse the mortal quality of the human organism with the immortality of the Person, since Person (here spelled with a capital) is not the same as nature. Person should be distinguished from the nature in which it is incarnated. The union of Person and nature is not dualistic in the sense that Person and nature are two "things." They are rather two co-activities or dynamisms working as a single unit. Nature is assumed by the person and irradiated by it, like a luminous crystal whose light source emanates from a mysterious center within. Taken as a whole, the light that illumines and the illumined are but a single reality. Though material comparisons and analogies can be misleading when applied to spiritual realities, perhaps we might risk saying that just as two primary pigments, blue and yellow, when mixed together result in a single color, green, so the human and the divine, Person and nature are but a single theandric reality.

For Plato, the human Person (*psyche,* or soul) is *of its very nature* immortal. It cannot go out of existence or come into existence. It cannot begin to be. Theologians make a distinction between change properly so called and change in an improper sense. Properly speaking, change occurs in an already existing entity or subject which loses or acquires some property, accident, or quality. The fat man with curly hair becomes thin and bald. Change in the improper sense would be creation out of nothing: there would be no preexisting subject out of which or within which the new being came into existence. There is a third possibility, however. It stands somewhere between ordinary change and creation out of nothing. This is what I call latency.

Latency

When a female child is born, she is already equipped with all the reproductive cells or ova she will ever have. They will not develop into a new organism unless fertilized, but will remain latent. Similarly, I venture to suggest that the immortal human spirit or Person, before entering the spatio-temporal dimension, exists in a state which I shall now call preembryonic, that is, as a divine cell in the bosom of God. (And here, by the way, the image of God as Mother is more appropriate than that of

Father.) These divine seedlings or eggs exist outside time, so it would not be meaningful to ask "how long" they have existed in this latent state before assuming a body. Only when they incarnate in a body do these divine seedlings awaken, become fertile, and begin to acquire human experience, memories, and the kind of knowledge that can come only with bodily and brain-related existence and activity.

Time and space, the material media, are the soil in which the human Person germinates and develops reflexive consciousness. Prior to incarnation, the spirit existed in a transtemporal state beyond name and form in a kind of dreamless, paradisiacal latency. Since everything in God is divine, whether we regard human spirits as substantive divine ideas or as seminal, ovate entities, they share in the divine life and are images of their Parent. They flower in time and begin to actualize or realize their potentialities which would not have been awakened had they remained latent in God.

One of the passages in the Gospel of Matthew that goes almost unnoticed is that in which Jesus says of children that "their angels always see the face of God" (Matt. 18:10), or at least abide in the divine presence. In the Jewish scriptures angels are called spirits or breaths or winds. The "angel" or spirit of the Person may very well be what is deepest, most spiritual, and divine in each one of us, that aspect of our being that always abides in the divine presence and never leaves it. In the Fourth Gospel, Jesus says, "No one has ascended into heaven but the one who has descended from heaven, the Son of Man *who is in heaven*" (John 3:13). I would postulate that what is said of Jesus is true of all of us. Some aspect of our incarnate being is always in heaven, has never left it.

Wordsworth captured this thought in his ode "Intimations of Immortality from Recollections of Early Childhood":

> Our birth is but a sleep and a forgetting:
> The Soul that rises with us, our life's Star,
> Hath had elsewhere its setting,
> And cometh from afar:
> Not in entire forgetfulness,
> And not in utter nakedness,
> But trailing clouds of glory do we come
> From God who is our home:
> Heaven lies about us in our infancy!

To begin to experience the divine presence within us, is the first step on the return journey home.

What about Sin?

On the purely natural level and in biological terms, we are mammals and members of the order of primates. We share 98 percent of our genes with the higher apes. Thus we are equipped with inborn animal instincts. At that level, we, as a species, are inclined to behave pretty much as other predatory animals. Individuals and groups protect their territory with aggressive or evasive actions, and because the earth's resources are limited, we are inclined to accumulate goods and wealth in order to survive and to survive in comfort. This reflects nature's way. When uncontrolled, these instincts degenerate into human greed and injustice. Those who live purely natural lives live by those familiar maxims that reflect the self-centered outlook.

Alongside the drive for self-aggrandizement at the expense of others there is a struggling, nascent form of altruism. It is found in some animals and in primitive humans, although its exercise is usually limited to the welfare of the brood, clan, or tribe. But even in the purely natural order human beings do on occasion make sacrifices for others. When intelligence is concerned, this may only be a form of enlightened self-interest, but at least it does provide a counterbalance to unrestrained selfishness. The fact remains, however, that, as Wilfred Trotter noted in the early part of this century, humans are herding animals.[11] This is noticeable at all ages, but is especially prominent in the adolescent years. While youngsters in their teens may rebel against parental authority, they readily yield to peer pressure. To be accepted into the group, one must conform to the social mores of the young set one aspires to belong to, whether this means in the kind of clothing one wears, the hairstyle one chooses, or the mannerisms one cultivates. This creates the sense of belonging. It may turn out to be innocent enough, or it may lead to antisocial behavior, everything from group rape to mindless vandalism. It is reminiscent of the herding instinct.

Not just young people, but even adults will do in a group what they would not dare do as individuals. Mob psychology takes over when, like sharks in a feeding frenzy, male hoodlums destroy property, assault defenseless individuals, and even kill. These same people on a one-to-one basis often seem to be mild, even insecure, people. One of the ideas which military trainers seek to inculcate the world over is that the enemy is less than human. If the soldier is sufficiently brainwashed with this demonizing message drummed into him, he will find it easier to kill and

---

11. *The Instinct of the Herd in Peace and War* (London, 1916).

even torture the enemy. Nazi storm troopers were trained, like dogs in obedience school, to hate Jews. The same men who were devoted fathers and husbands were able to herd Jews into boxcars, drive them into extinction camps, starve and kill them, then go home and fondle the dog and play with the children.

What intelligence and human freedom add to raw animal instinct is the ability to find exquisite ways of satisfying these instincts, whether it is a question of the domination of others, the exercise of power, kinky sex, grand larceny, mail fraud or, of course, warfare.

Conversion

These are extreme cases of the burden that most of us carry with us as part of our evolutionary inheritance. The story of the Fall historicizes what theologians call our flawed human nature. But Adam and Eve are not two people who sinned in the recent past, some six thousand years ago, and got the human race off to a bad start. The Fall represents the distance between the ideal we are called to realize and the way we actually do behave. We are not so much a fallen race as one with a vocation to transcend our animal instincts. "Sin" is the word we use to describe the extent of our failure to measure up to the dignity of our calling.

We all need to have the experience of conversion. It may occur only gradually, all of a sudden, or not at all. Conversion takes place when we take responsibility for our thoughts and actions and strive to overcome the drives of our animal past enhanced by reason. In biblical language this is called a change of mind and heart, or *metanoia*. It is often translated into English as "repent." When Jesus, following John the Baptist, came calling for repentance (Mark 1:15), his appeal was addressed to all in need of reform. St. Paul universalizes the ubiquity of sin when he says, "For there is no distinction, since all have sinned and fall short of the glory of God" (Rom. 3:23). As I said earlier, I have some reservations about the universality of sin. While virtually all people have their faults and imperfections, I do believe there are some who maintain their innocence throughout life, never doing anything that can be said to offend God. Others, after early lapses, achieve a state of true sinless holiness.

The call for repentance need not imply the total corruption of nature and a guilt inherited from a pair of wayward ancestors. It simply reminds us that we are finite beings, capable of error in ordinary life situations as well as in moral matters. Socrates held that if we thoroughly understood how we are demeaned and diminished by unjust actions, we would find it all but impossible to commit them. What people in the West call sin, those in the East, Hindus and Buddhists, attribute to ignorance. Most ancient manuscripts of Luke's Gospel include Jesus' prayer to his Father, asking the Father to forgive those responsible for his death, "for they do not know what they are doing" (Luke 23:34). This again calls attention to the element of ignorance involved in most blameworthy acts.

Awakening from Ignorance

Conversion, then, is largely a matter of perceiving the error of one's ways and of reorienting one's energies in the direction of improvement. This can take place whether one believes in God or not. A reasonably intelligent person can one day find that leading an aimless or dissolute life does not lead to personal satisfaction and contentment. Here one's rational nature and freedom of choice are employed to overcome the disordered instincts of nature. A housecleaning of this kind is almost always a prerequisite for advancing higher. The supernatural order builds on nature, provided the latter is not too untamed.

The Gospel, as good news, speaks to the innermost core of our being, reminding us that we are much more than animals who happen to be rational. It informs us that we have a supernatural destiny and that the human spirit cannot go out of existence. "For this perishable body must put on imperishability, and this mortal body must put on immortality" (1 Cor. 15:53). Each of us is a sacred shrine, harboring the immortal self, something that totally transcends the perishable body with its appetites. As one enters into this new awareness, the superior appetites or instincts begin to replace or overrule the lower ones. We are attracted by the lure of goodness and the beauty of God. In privileged moments, what had seemed so attractive to the "natural man" now seems as unreal as a dream.

The proper function of preaching is to awaken in the hearer a lively awareness of this other, transcendent dimension of our constitution. This is not something that we *acquire* by faith and grace. Rather it is faith and grace that enables us to *realize* our true nature as divine offspring. Being born again or from above (John 3:3–4) assumes that one has already been conceived in the eternal womb of God. Achieving this awareness comes at the end of a threefold awakening. The first stage on the road to enlightenment is reached when a narrow and self-enclosed dedication to satisfying one's lower appetites is modified by a rudimentary kind of altruism, or at least by enlightened self-interest. The second stage is attained when there is a genuine change of heart or conversion away from the inclination to yield to self-centered interests and the need to serve one's personal convenience at the expense of others. This opens the way for the third stage. It includes the realization and conviction that we are divine offspring, sharing in the divine nature, that we are temples of the Holy Spirit, that others also share in this dignity. We are still fallible, still capable of thoughtless acts of unkindness, of feelings of self-importance, and of moments of impatience. But in spite of occasional lapses, all our desire is for God and the welfare of others. This is the Life Divine.

"Participants of the Divine Nature" (2 Pet. 1:4)

To say that someone shares in divinity — a perfectly orthodox Christian statement — does not feel quite the same as if one were to say that John or Mary is God. It even feels a bit awkward when applied to the divinity of Christ. Jesus did not go about saying, "I am God," though John in the Fourth Gospel says that he was. To share in the divine nature, or to be in some sense divine, does not mean that the individual is the creator and uncaused cause of all that is. No one can be God in the sense in which God is God, since even an eternal being other than God would have to stand in a relationship of dependence on God for its being and continued existence. Nevertheless, insofar as we share in the divine nature, it is not incorrect to use the adjectival form and say that, viewed comprehensively, there is a divine element in every human being, that it is an essential part of our constitution, not something added to it.

So, as indicated above, this means that we are immortal. But since the human body does deteriorate and die, what is immortal is that aspect of our being that exists independent of time and space. This means independent of the temporal sequence of before and after, of past and future. This logically implies that the human Person neither ceases to exist nor begins to exist, since a "beginning" implies time. This eternal existence, both before and after incarnation, does not rule out dependence. The human life principles, sperm and ovum, depend for their existence on the existence of the bodies of men and women that secrete them. Human spirits in their virtual or latent state as *aiōnia*, eternal seedlings in the bosom of God, gestate and come to maturity in the soil of time. In other words, their latent potentialities begin to flower when they enter time. Then, after passing a number of years in the temporal dimension, they return to the source whence they came, rich with incarnational experience.

We thus come from God and return to God, bringing with us what 1 Peter calls the "imperishable seed" (1 Pet. 1:23). John the Evangelist speaks of those who were "born of God [*ek theou egennēthēsan*]" (John 1:13). In both 1 Peter and John the impression is given that the divine nature is something that is acquired in the course of a lifetime through faith in Jesus. As already pointed out, what is questionable is whether one "acquires" the divine status through faith and grace, as an onto-logical condition, or whether the ontological condition already exists, so that the role of faith and grace is to enable us to become cognizant of, that is, realize our true nature as divine offspring. This comes close to the doctrine taught in the Upanishads in India: The unborn self, the *Atman,* is neither born nor does it die. While an avatar is a special incar-nation of God, every ordinary human Person shares in the divine nature. Or, stated more baldly, the essence of the self is to be "That." *Atman* (the self) is *Brahman* (the divine ground of being): *Tat tvam asi.*[12]

Can this be harmonized with traditional Christian teaching concern-ing the participation of the human Person in the divine nature? The more obvious and literal sense of the New Testament would seem to require that what is conceived in accord with the laws of nature — conceived in the state of Original Sin — can be saved and share in the divine life only through faith in Christ. Divinity, then, is something ac-quired through the sacrificial death of Jesus and communicated through his grace by means of faith. Since the vast majority of people alive to-day on this planet are not Christians and have no inclination to accept Jesus as their personal savior, theologians who were uncomfortable with the kind of exclusivism that regarded such nonbelievers as lost sought a way to allow that salvation might be possible outside the confines of Christianity. So we hear of the "Anonymous Christian," people saved by implicit faith in what Jesus stands for or by a baptism of desire.

It would be simpler if Christian theologians took seriously the first chapter of the Book of Genesis, where it is stated plainly that God made humankind to God's own image and likeness (Gen. 1:26). This is an image that can be covered over and obscured, but never lost. It is an endowment which every child born of woman enjoys. To be like God, in God's likeness, is not a metaphor but a statement of fact. We are That. To *be* it and to *realize* it are two different things. So while some passages in the New Testament convey the idea that we become godlings only by

---

12. *Chandogya Upanishad* VI, 10–16.

explicit faith in the man Jesus, others strongly suggest that we are all divine offspring and true children of God and that the Gospel, the good news, is the revelation that this is who we are, saints and sinners alike. The role of the savior is to help people discover their true identity and act out the implications of their divine calling.

The Super*natural*

In tribal societies, the name of the in-group or clan very often means, in its language, "humankind" or "people." Bears, wolves, and foxes are, obviously, not people. But this designation of nonhumanity is also extended to members of a neighboring tribe. "They are not like us; so they aren't really people, not quite human." When the stranger speaks a different language or looks different, the we-they dichotomy becomes even more pronounced. As a result, these "others" become fair game and can be hunted and killed like any other nonhuman animal. If an alliance is made with a neighboring tribe for defensive or aggressive purposes, the former enemies now become people.

Just how extensively this "We, the People" feeling can be stretched varies, but it rarely becomes so broad that it includes every member of the human race. If several tribes form an alliance, this is usually based on the perception of a community of interests. In other words, it is an example of enlightened self-interest. This is one step above single-tribe exclusivism and is the product of intelligence. It is not yet moral. The latter involves doing what is right, whether it is of advantage to the agent or not. For example, an elderly couple with no children might vote for an increase in local taxes to pay for the refurbishing of a neighborhood elementary school and playground for the welfare of other people's children. The couple support the tax because they are able to empathize with the needs of others in the community. Another childless couple might vote against the tax because they have no children and improving the school offers no immediate personal advantage.

The moral order lies midway between raw nature and what is truly supernatural. Unlike the instinctive forms of altruism found in some animals, morality includes an intelligent, free decision based on a norm which is either adhered to or spurned. What the moral application is may differ from culture to culture, but ethical conduct always implies deliberate choice in relation to an ideal or goodness that is acceptable in one's community. Of course, there is an element of contingency that must be taken into consideration, since what might be morally acceptable in one society could be regarded as immoral in another. It is only when the individual person is perceived as sharing in the divine life that the inviolability of other persons can be solidly grounded. This perception applies to young and old, male and female, regardless of race, creed, or color. Here reason is not enough, whether it is "enlightened" or based on sound moral principles. "Do unto others as you would have them do unto you," is a noble maxim, and it does indicate an ability to put oneself in the other person's place, but it is not yet supernatural. It is not based on a deep perception of the divinity of the other person as, therefore, inviolable. This perception is adumbrated in the strict interpretation of the two commandments Jesus cited when referring to Deuteronomy 6:5 in connection with Leviticus 19:18: The love of neighbor is inseparable from the love of God (Matt. 22:37–39). The First Epistle of John adds flesh to this teaching: If you are unable to love your neighbor whom you can see, how will you manage to love God whom you can't see? (1 John 4:20). The neighbor is our visible God.

What one has to be able to "see" is the aspect of divinity which we all share, whether the neighbor is insane, physically or mentally handicapped, criminally inclined, or as yet unborn. Speaking as or for God, Jesus declares that whatever is done to injure or assist the least among men or women is, in fact, done unto him. Done, that is, to what he is, namely, true Son of God (Matt. 25:40). By the same token, if another person injures or assists me, he or she is affecting the divine presence that I incarnate.

Arrogance or Humility?

It might seem unseemly and presumptuous to arrogate to oneself qualities that belong to God alone. It is true that only God is God, but it is equally true that human beings do participate in the divine life. To participate means to have a share in. And since the divine life is not divisible, to share in it does not mean to have only a "piece" of it. The divinity is present, whole and entire, housed in mortal flesh. St. Paul speaks of the body as a temple of the Holy Spirit. "Do you not know that you are God's temple and that God's Spirit dwells in you? ... For God's temple is holy and you are that temple" (1 Cor. 3:16). Since the body is eventually sloughed off, what remains is the immortal, divine Spirit or self. The complement to recognizing this in another is the ability to recognize it in oneself. What this recognition should engender in us is not satanic pride but humility and gratitude. What possible return

could one give back to God for such a gift? When one is completely secure in knowing who one is, there is no need for pretense or posturing.
Even persons fully aware of their inadequacies and faults will be inspired
to lead more saintly lives if they can manage to realize their true dignity
as divine offspring, born of God. It is when people fail to respect themselves that they begin to put on airs, in order to convince others and
themselves that they are worthwhile and significant persons. Fully realized people have no need of this. At the other end of the spectrum are
those whose self-image is so poor that they despise themselves and their
own shadow. How could they dare assume that they are anything but
trash? So why pretend to be, or aspire to act like, divine offspring?

Jesus challenges them as he challenges each one of us to recognize
our intrinsic worth. Aware of our own dignity and that of others, we
would find it impossible to injure another person or abuse ourselves and
the temple of flesh in which we dwell. Rather, we would be eager to use
our talents, however slight, so that the light that is in us may radiate
the divine goodness and contribute to improving the quality of life for
at least one other person on this small planet.

Chapter 16

RESURRECTION AND IMMORTALITY

I would like in this chapter to pursue several strands of thought touched on in the previous chapter, especially the idea that the great "gift of God" is immortality. But maybe you don't want to live forever. At least not in this outfit which you call your mortal body. It wears out — or haven't you noticed? Dying has always happened to other people, so far. But eventually it will be our turn.

There are people who believe in total extinction after death; others who do not, but who do not look forward to living on forever and ever and ever. Won't it be boring, even if one is free from all pain and sorrow? Many people — racing drivers, mountain climbers — would rather risk their young lives than be bored staying at home. Anyhow, who knows what being dead is like? Who has really been there and returned to tell about it?

Most people, especially the young, are not vividly aware of their mortality. Time marches on at a slow pace when one is in elementary school or suffering through the teens; it gallops as one passes the meridian of life. Ten years ago seems like yesterday. As the body deteriorates, one has the feeling an old-time aviator must have had as his flying machine began to fall apart in midair. First a strut falls off, then a wheel. Then the wing begins to shred. So far only the pilot remains intact, at least for the time being. He is not the plane, but the plane is undeniably his life support system while aloft. So, too, is the body our support system while we are down here. As it begins to shred and our memory for what happened an hour ago blurs, one cannot help wondering what, if anything, comes next. Next, that is, after physical death.

Most of the world's religious scriptures assure us that what comes next is vastly superior to what goes on here, that is, if you're a half-decent sort. But does a belief in the survival of the person after death really make any difference? Preachers use fear of punishment as a stick to scare people into being good. It probably doesn't produce any lasting results beyond helping a few exemplary pew holders feel guilty. It also portrays God as primarily a punisher. But why demonize God under a cloak of "justice"? If we, poor humans, are supposed to forgive our enemies seventy times seven times, is God to be regarded as less than human?

Immortality can make a difference in one's attitude toward God, if we learn to appreciate what a gift it is. Deep down, nobody really wants to go out of business as far as existing, knowing, and loving are concerned. Even an ant tries to preserve its life if you try to step on it. The instinct for living on is translated in human terms into a desire to live on forever. The difference between humans and animals is that humans do know that they are going to die, and this does influence our behavior to some extent. We take out life insurance to protect our loved ones. Animals do not. Philosopher Martin Heidegger defined Man as a "being unto death." His point is that no matter how carefree we may pretend to be, in the back of our minds there is always the realization of our mortality. Historically, there have been two ways of responding to this realization: drain as much pleasure out of life as you can, or do not cling to these things since they are impermanent.

Narrow escapes and near-death experiences have a way of sobering one's attitude toward life. Most of those who have had a profound NDE no longer fear death, and, while still in the flesh, they find the present life increasingly rich and meaningful. They seek to make the most of the time remaining to them by a life of service for others and devotion to God. They have gone through something like death and know that it is only a rite of passage to a much larger universe.

The Testimony of the Mystics

Another source that should impart confidence to those who have not had a near-death encounter is the fact that the great mystics in all the world's religions have, during their peak experiences, entered into something like the experience of eternity. They come back *knowing* that the human spirit is immortal, that it will not, indeed cannot, die. What takes place in a truly ecstatic state resembles to some degree the experience of death. The somatic and psychic systems of the organism slow down so that they are all but indiscernible even when tested with instruments under laboratory conditions. St. Paul, speaking of this kind of state, said that it is hard to know whether one is in the body or out of it (2 Cor. 12:2). On such occasions, one has moved out of this world into a completely different dimension of reality. So, like NDEers, authentic mystics do not believe in immortality. They know.

There is another kind of mystical state which does not involve physiological changes. It is always open to the pure of heart. Here, one is wide awake, more awake than in the most alert state of consciousness. Often, without any preparation a person suddenly seems to see through a material form to the ocean of loving goodness that is self-expressing in and through the cloud or flower or the saintly person one meets. Even the achievements of humankind, so gifted by God with intelligence, can induce a spirit of adoring wonder. Most amazing of all is the fact of one's own existence, the fact that one is conscious of being conscious, that prior to and beyond anything I can have — be it power, money, friends, a body, even a soul — I am. It is the "I" that has and is not had. Its very nature is to be and to be eternally.

This kind of unprovoked realization can be stunning. It is the sort of peak experience which brings peace and an influx of unearthly joy. For some, the experience is almost too much, and they have to weep for joy. Beyond the immediate realization is the deeper insight into the divine immensity and the boundless love of God which surpasses all understanding. Why would a benevolent creator provide humans with such experiences and the conviction of eternal life if the experiences and the desire were a complete deception. That would be the cruelest joke of all.

What's It Like?

The best analogy we can come up with to describe eternal life or immortality is to compare it with the way time evaporates when we are happy and enjoying some moving experience. You are engaged, for example, in reading an absorbing book. The time slips by so rapidly that you forget to eat. Or you are attending a great dramatic production, enraptured by the sound of a great singer, or given only a few minutes to bid farewell to a sweetheart. What all these experiences have in common is that time flies. I call it the Cinderella Effect. She went to the ball and was so absorbed in the music and dancing that when midnight came it seemed as though only a few minutes had passed since she had first come to the prince's palace. On such joyful occasions one almost loses a sense of self to become totally immersed in the event. We often speak of a person being lost in thought or carried away by a powerful esthetic experience. Time contracts almost to an instant, or its moments are so telescoped together that the beginning and the end are as one. One is no longer aware of the body. Even if a person had been suffering from a very painful injury or disease, in such moments the pain is forgotten and the gross material world seems far away.

So we can experience a mystical state either by closing off the outer world entirely, so that one is all but dead to the world; or we may have an intense and arresting cognitive and affective experience by losing ourselves in the wonder and beauty of an object or person. What is common to both experiences is that our everyday occupation with the small ego-self disappears. Not that that self has become extinct, but it can have no share in the pie. Its role, as a coping device or psychological mechanism, is to help us survive in a dangerous world. But when we enter into eternal life or its momentary intimations, it is simply quiescent. As we return to ordinary consciousness it will come back to life again, as it must, and for a short time we may feel like aliens in an alien land. It may be that heaven is nothing more complicated than a total forgetfulness of self! People given to the selfless service of others may already be there without knowing it.

You Can't Merit It

St. Paul said that "no eye has seen, nor ear heard, nor the human heart conceived what God has prepared for those who love him" (1 Cor. 2:9). Paul, who was both an ecstatic and a tireless apostle, knew whereof he spoke. What God has prepared far exceeds anything the senses can feel, the mind conceive, or the heart desire. When Jesus speaks of eternal life in John's Gospel, he is not simply referring to continued existence but to the kind of life God enjoys. It is called a gift because it cannot be merited, not even as a quid pro quo in exchange for good behavior. Deservingness has nothing to do with God's free gifts, including the fact of our own conscious existence.

That is the real point of that parable which gives some people so much trouble. I mean the one about the laborers in the vineyard (Matt. 20:1–16). Those who were hired in the morning and worked all day got the same pay as those who began work at the last minute just before quitting time. The last to come got a day's wage; those who came early and worked all day received the same pay. The parable is really not about earthly wages but about divine gifts. If a man lives to be ninety and dies and finds that his spirit is immortal in God's presence, should he be grieved if he learns that a ten-year-old who just died has been granted the same eternal life and immortality? To such a person the Lord might ask, as in the parable, "Are you envious because I am generous?" (Matt. 20:15). What belongs to God by nature is immortality and divinity. If God shares them with those who die young as well as with the old, should we be upset? Or would you rather see your worst enemies die and become extinct or, even better, would you have them survive death and go to hell for all eternity? Such an attitude measures the gap between the mind of Christ and some of us in our darkest moments.

Continuous Progress

Is human life a once-around-the-block affair? Eastern religions offer the alternative of some form of reincarnation. It is not dogma, but it presents a possible explanation for a number of things, including the suffering of the innocent and the presence of evil, especially the evils perpetrated by human beings. The Law of Karma represents a kind of cosmic justice: As you sow, so shall you reap. Each successive incarnation provides an opportunity to learn and to move up higher on the scale of perfection until, at last, one escapes the wheel of *samsara*. This is graduation day and one to be sought after and looked forward to. Only the Bodhisattva is willing to postpone leaving the terrestrial plane until every living thing has been redeemed out of time.

Traditional Christianity has held to the single life opportunity. We pass this way only once. For those less than perfect but by no means wicked, Catholicism introduced the in-between stage of Purgatory. Eventually, after a "time" of purification in Purgatory, all will be released and enter the state of eternal bliss. Purgatory fell into disrepute at the time of the Reformation because of the sale of indulgences, which featured the promotional idea that, if a person made a donation to a holy cause (often a political one in disguise), one would have so many days cut off one's future assignment in Purgatory. Setting aside the puerility connected with the idea of celestial bookkeeping, the concept of continued progress after death is not without merit.

Behind this assumption is the idea that the human spirit not only survives death but also has unending opportunities to grow in wisdom and grace. That remarkably perceptive early Father of the Church Gregory of Nyssa held that after death progress goes on indefinitely "from glory to glory." At the moment of death one is not frozen into an inalterable posture like Lot's wife; for, since God is infinitely intelligible, there can be no limit to the spirit's opportunity to expand endlessly into the boundless richness of the divine life.

The space-time world we are familiar with is in all probability among the lowest in a much larger universe of higher levels of being. It was only in relatively recent times that it was discovered that visible light constitutes but a very narrow band in the full electromagnetic spectrum, which ranges from very long radio waves to X-rays and gamma rays. As with the material world, so also with the world of the spirit. There is no reason why the world of visible and measurable objects need be the only one. Jesus said, "In my Father's house there are many dwelling places" (John 14:2). I take this to mean both that one's spiritual progress continues after death and that many people drawn from all the world's religions will have dwelling places in the eternal kingdom.

How High Is Up?

In passing from glory to glory, from one stage of beatitude to a higher, St. John of the Cross offers the image of a fagot of wood moving closer and closer to the divine Fire. Then suddenly at one particular stage the chip of wood bursts into flames to become ablaze and indistinguishable from the divine Fire. The only reason why the wood could catch fire is because it is already dark, imprisoned fire itself. What I mean is that I do not think any entity can be transubstantiated into the divine, unless it is already in some sense what it will become in a more explicit way. St. Paul says that he considered that "the sufferings of this present time are not worthy to be compared with the *glory* that shall be revealed in us [or to us: *eis hēmas*]" (Rom. 8:18). Throughout the New Testament salvation means participating in the divine life. It is something one internally and eternally shares in, and is.

Depending on whether one chooses to follow a nondual or a dualist interpretation of what it means for persons to be divine "offspring" (Acts 17:28), "born of God" (John 1:13), or "partakers of the divine nature" (2 Pet. 1:4), one will hold that the human spirit is gifted with the divine life as constitutive of its natural endowment or subsequently gifted after birth with it as something added to a rational human nature. In the mid-1940s Henri de Lubac, the illustrious Jesuit theologian, in his book, *Surnaturel: études historiques* (1946), attacked the idea that the human being's supernatural destiny was a gift *added to* our rational human nature. De Lubac never denied that the Beatific Vision and participation in the divine life were gifts, but in the concrete, historical order a purely "natural" human being never existed. We are created in the image and likeness of God, and our absolute, ineradicable de-

sire for God (*desiderium naturale* in the idiom of St. Thomas) stems
from our nature as the image of God. De Lubac, because of the oppo-
sition of a few conservative theologians (including some of his Jesuit
brethren), did not spell out the full implications of his position and
say that there is an exigency in the human being for the supernatural
fulfillment of human life by the very fact that we are divine offspring
and images of God, therefore truly children of God, constitutionally an
incorruptible seed.

Were de Lubac's thesis expanded beyond what he was willing to declare, it would approximate the nondual position which holds that the
human Person, incarnated in a rational human nature, is essentially divine in a seminal way, as a tiny seedling shares in the nature of the
full-grown tree. For the dualist, divinization comes to a rational human
nature, which was in no sense divine to start with but was divinized
through faith by an act of God, an act comparable to creation.

Both the nondual and the dualist positions have difficulties. If we are
seminally divine, how does it happen that we are not aware of so great
a gift? Or, looking at it from the dualist point of view, if one only becomes divine, or is divinized, for example, at the time of baptism, the
same question can be asked as above. How is it that we are not aware
of it? Is it possible to be not divine at one moment and a minute later
become divine, or can one gradually become divine, being only semidi-
vine along the way? Finally, if only those who become divine in the
course of their lifetime will see God and enjoy eternal life, what is to become of the 4.8 billion people on planet earth (roughly 80 percent of the
world's population) who are not Christians; therefore not divinized by
faith and baptism, with the consequence that they are eternally excluded
from the beatific vision of God, not to mention even more disastrous
consequences for their life in the world to come?

Somewhere along the way common sense ought to prevail. We are
either "trailing clouds of glory" or we are dust bins pretending to be
something. Being seminally but truly divine is a position which eliminates many of the logical conundrums that the strict dualist position
entails. The Psalmist may have said it as well as anyone. "You [God]
have made them [humans] a little lower than yourself" (Ps. 8:5). Some
translations render this as, "a little lower than the angels" — seen as
divine beings. The RSV renders this phrase as, "a little lower than God."

Without trying to specify too precisely just what participation in the
divine nature means, we can say that there is more in each one of us
than rationality joined to animality. Our Person shares in one of the
prerogatives of divinity, namely, immortality. The Greeks and Romans

were conscious of this when they spoke of their gods as "the immortals." For them divinity and immortality were all but synonymous. Or, to put it another way, what is immortal is in some sense divine. Plato used many arguments to demonstrate that the soul is immortal and indestructible. It is not just a question of surviving the dissolution of the body but of its inability to not-exist or become extinct. And just as the human spirit cannot cease being immortal, neither can it begin to be immortal. When we say that it always was and always will be, using the past and future tenses, we are condemned to using timebound language. The human Person or spirit simply is; it is an "I am," not a was or a will be. In its existence it is essentially independent of time.

"What Dreams May Come"

The opposite of eternal life is not eternal death or extinction. The human spirit cannot go out of existence. But it stands to reason that a soul estranged from God by inhuman acts will not experience nontemporal existence or eternity the way the just do, at least not right away. Clinging to such a soul will be the vestiges of time misspent, minus the kind of distractions possible in the embodied state. I suspect that what constitutes a kind of hell is not physical pain or even the anguish of a guilt-ridden memory, but sheer boredom and monotony; in other words, empty time. Sometimes in dream states we keep coming back to the same inconclusive and frustrating patterns, as though haunted by fragments of the past, by memories that keep recurring like the ghosts that are said to haunt certain places on earth.

Shakespeare's Hamlet had a positive fear of survival and immortality. In the famous soliloquy beginning with "To be or not to be," Hamlet was not afraid of dying or being killed. He feared what might lie beyond death for a man about to commit murder:

> To sleep! perchance to dream: — ay, there's the rub;
> For in the sleep of death what dreams may come,
> When we have shuffled off this mortal coil,
> Must give us pause. . . . (Act III, scene 1)

We create our own hells and purgatories by the way we live and by the things we do. There must be some kind of growth in eternity even for the most wicked. The Buddhists have many hells and a number of overhead heavens. People can live in them temporarily in this life as well as in the next, but no one is cemented into any one of them. Eventually the divine light and love must penetrate even the blackest, thickest darkness. Too many sermons and revival meetings have dwelt on guilt and the absorbing subject of the exquisite tortures of hell. It is a tempting subject for a preacher with a lively and somewhat distorted imagination. Jonathan Edwards, an otherwise down-to-earth theologian in colonial times, is famous for his lurid sermons on hell. One was so vivid that members of his congregation fainted or became hysterical. It prompted me a number of years ago to sum him up in a limerick:

> The wages of sin were a feature
> Of Jonathan Edwards the teacher.
>   It was easy to tell
>   From his sermons on hell,
> He'd been there and come back to preach here.

Joseph Campbell, in *Creative Mythology,* the last of his four volumes in his Masks of God series, cites James Joyce's account of a typical retreat sermon (50–52), the kind preached to adolescent boys during the years when Joyce was in school as a youth in Dublin. It would begin with the benign retreat master lecturing his young charges with genuine solicitude: "Now let us try for a moment to realize, as far as we can, the nature of the abode of the damned which the justice of an offended God has called into existence for the eternal punishment of sinners. Hell is a strait and dark foulsmelling prison.... Not only are the senses marvelously tortured by the officiating minions of Satan, but this will go on forever and ever without end or respite." There is no evidence in such an account of the Good Shepherd who will not rest until he has saved the most wayward of his charges. The sinner is stuck for millions and billions of earth years without reprieve or any possible alteration or improvement in this hopeless condition. Strange god, indeed. One made in the image of our own vindictive nature and likeness. It turns immortality into a curse and makes God the arch-torturer, acting vicariously through demon deputies.

Resurrection

The creeds speak of "the resurrection of the dead, and life in the world to come." The resurrection of Jesus is seen as the model for the eventual resurrection of all. But, if Jesus returned to his tomb and reanimated his corpse some thirty-six hours after his burial, he had the advantage of having at his disposal an already existing and intact body with its organs still in place and ready to be put in working condition upon the return of its owner.

No such convenience awaits those who died many centuries ago, all of whose bodies have returned to dust and to the chemicals of which they were composed. This planet is a vast cemetery, cradling the bones and ashes of humans and prehumans over millions of years. If the resurrection means getting back one's original body as Jesus is said to have done, there is going to be a wild scramble on the Last Day as billions of the deceased look for the original elements, or reasonable facsimiles, of their once mortal bodies.

Such a scene is, of course, close to comedy. To make any sense at all, a risen "body" must not be made of meat and molecules. St. Paul saw the difficulty when he spoke of two kinds of body: the corruptible one and the incorruptible one. "If there is a physical body, there is also a spiritual body" (1 Cor. 15:44). In the oriental traditions, there is mention of several different kinds of bodies, sometimes called the somatic, the ethereal, and the astral bodies. They are nested "inside" one another, like Chinese boxes. When one dissolves and falls away, another is found inside it, until only the most subtle and refined body remains. This one is imperishable.

For the Christian, what does the resurrection add to survival and immortality? It means the reappropriation of the significance of one's experience in time. The mere survival of the individual is not enough. One's excursion into time would be pointless if the surviving individual did not assimilate all that had been learned and undergone from birth to death. People who have near-death experiences often have their whole life pass before them in a matter of seconds. What they perceive, whether good or bad, whether once painful or pleasant, is viewed dispassionately and objectively without a sense of harrowing guilt or undue elation.

What recovers and relives these memory events — at least for a while, until the spirit has moved on to more universal, less circumscribed concerns — is not a bare *res cognitans* but a center of consciousness housed in a spiritual vehicle or pneumatic body by means of which it is able to communicate and express itself to others. One of the purposes of the *postresurrection* appearances of Jesus was to demonstrate that the risen Person is not something like an animated abstract idea but a concrete reality, though not a grossly material one.

In Virgil's *Aeneid,* when Aeneas and his faithful crew were undergoing various hardships on their way to found the city of Rome, Aeneas said to his sailors, "The day will come when it will be a joy to remem-

ber these things," meaning these trials and adventures. Memory purifies
the past, leaving only the filtered essence of all that has been suffered. It
allows us to see everything as a series of stages leading up to the present.
It takes the sting out of the unpleasant and the ugly and casts into relief
the good and the true. Above all and at its best, it forgives.

I do not know what happened to the *physical* body of Jesus. What
rose from the dead or, more accurately, never died at all is what Paul
calls the pneumatic body, one no longer enclosed in the physical body
and subject to the limitations of time and space. It could appear to
the Emmaus-bound disciples, disappear, and moments later reappear to
Peter back in Jerusalem.

It is not the case that the resurrection of Jesus made life after death
possible. The major religions have taught from earliest times that the
human spirit survives physical death in one fashion or another. Long
before the time of Jesus the Persians and Hindus knew of survival. Plato
had no doubt about immortality. Since the spirit is without parts, it
cannot disintegrate or fall apart.

Even so, the resurrection is a *revelation*. It not only dispels any doubt
about human survival after death, but it is also a guarantee that Persons
will not lose their uniqueness and be reabsorbed into the infinite ground
of being. Just as the material body was the principle of individuation
by which a multitude of incarnate rational creatures retained their distinctness from one another in the space-time medium, so the spiritual or
pneumatic body serves as the principle of individuation or individuality
by which risen Persons retain their uniqueness and distinctness from one
another, along with a permeability and a capacity for mutual indwelling
which a gross material body does not have.

I said that Jesus rose from the dead at the moment of his death on the
cross. Between that moment and the disappearance of his material body
from the tomb, he is said, according to 1 Peter, to have been already
"alive in the spirit" (3:19) and, as the creed puts it, to have "descended
into hell," that is, to the realm of deceased Persons. There he proclaimed
the good news, the kerygma *(ekēryxen)*, to those who were awaiting his
coming.

So Jesus was not "dead" during the thirty-six hours during which his
lifeless body lay in the tomb, but very much alive and active, already
risen in his pneumatic or spiritual body. I do not believe, as St. Paul
seems to suggest in 1 Thessalonians (4:15–17), that the dead hibernate
in a dreamless sleep and will awaken to conscious life only when Christ
returns to earth in glory many thousands of years from now. With the
author of the Fourth Gospel, I see the real resurrection and glorification

of Jesus taking place on the cross when he breathed his last. And I see his becoming "alive in the spirit" at the moment of his death as paradigmatic for all those who, having shed their mortal bodies, begin life anew in their spiritual bodies at the moment of death. For death is a birthing process which ends in a transfigured life in an immortal body.

Chapter 17

THE UNITY OF
CONTEMPLATIVE EXPERIENCE

Secular culture is a juggernaut, a powerful force. Like an irresistible tidal wave it sweeps everything before it. In light of the extension of industrialism and the capitalistic system to the nations of the Far East, including China, these countries are rapidly improving the quality of life for at least some of their more fortunate opportunists. But this kind of material progress has simultaneously served to erode many revered religious traditions that have been in place for thousands of years.

In an environment which is so unreservedly this-worldly, it is irrelevant to debate about whose religion is best or which is the only true one. The sides are clearly drawn between those who seek first the kingdom of God and those whose god is power, prestige, and material possessions. In this confrontation between spirituality and secularity, the devout Hindu, the practicing Buddhist, Moslem, Jew, or Christian are all ranged on the same side. Within the Christian community itself denominational differences, which at one time strictly separated baptized members of the various churches, are becoming less divisive. What is of greater importance than creedal differences is a commitment to moral integrity and the cultivation of an interior life with its overflow in charitable works of mercy supported by legislation that favors them.

This, after all, is the essence of Jesus' program, and it can be doubted that he would care whether it was carried out by a Protestant, Catholic, or Orthodox Christian, by a Sufi or a Zen Buddhist. The religion of Jesus, his personal religion, may have evolved in a first-century Jewish context, but it was essentially generic and not sectarian.

Presence versus Proselytism

Thoughtful Christians today who are familiar with other world religions are less inclined than in the past to trumpet the superiority of their own belief system over all others, even when they are deeply committed to their own path. While Christianity and Islam emphasize the importance of doctrine, creed, and scriptural inerrancy, Hinduism and Buddhism are more concerned with God-consciousness and religious experience. Each can learn from the others. When the late Dom Bede Griffiths went to India to live there for nearly forty years as a Christian sannyasin, or renunciate, he always remained a Christian monk and priest. He had not left England to convert the unenlightened heathen but to learn from the East. If those he befriended wished to learn about his Christian faith, he was there to accommodate them. Avoiding the "hard sell," which is so offensive to educated Hindus, he created an atmosphere of understanding and trust. There was little danger that he might become a Hindu, even though his lifestyle was like that of native holy men. Neither did he expect Hindus to turn Christian, though some did. Dom Bede had a profound respect for the deeper religious insights of India, and he was able to incorporate many of them into his own practice.

Jesus, who was concerned for the spiritual welfare of every living soul, did not range far beyond the boundaries of Palestine in an effort to convert Gentiles to his Jewish faith. But he was always available when Gentiles came to him. Still, humanly speaking, he might have been surprised to learn that his Jewish reform movement had turned into one of the major world religions, one centered on his person. St. Peter, standing on trial before the high priests and elders in Jerusalem, declared: "There is salvation in no one else, for there is no other name under heaven given among mortals by which we must be saved" (Acts 4:12).

Peter's designation of Jesus, the prophet from Nazareth, as the unique and indispensable savior of the whole world was not out of character. The people in the Jesus movement had an overpowering sense of their own election and destiny. And, in fact, Christianity turned into the mouse that roared; for in fewer than three centuries it became the official state religion of the entire Mediterranean world. Though Christianity lost members with the swift advance of Islam in the seventh century, whole nations were later won to the faith with the conversion of northern Europe and Russia. This was followed in the sixteenth century by the Christian colonization of the Americas.

Yet the fact remains that after almost two thousand years a bare fifth of the world's population can be regarded as even nominally Christian, and the fastest growing religion is Islam. Nevertheless, traces of the religion stemming from the teaching of Jesus, based on love, equality, and the works of mercy, have penetrated to most parts of the world. In this way, quite independent of whether a nation or its people converts to the Christian faith, the teaching of Jesus is a leaven that is at work in many places, even where the number of avowed Christians is negligible. By the same token, Eastern religious ideas and practices have of late penetrated to the West as never before. So the World is divided today, not so much between Christians and non-Christians as between people with high spiritual ideals on the one hand and secularity on the other, between God and mammon. What I understand by mammon is not just making an idol of money but the greedy pursuit of pleasure and material possession with little or no concern for the worship of God and gratitude for the gift of life.

All the major religions urge their adherents to try to overcome inordinate self love and seek those values that are imperishable rather than set their hearts on the transient values of this world. While Jesus speaks to the world as the Sacrament of God, that is, as the concrete embodiment of what God is like, he also shows us the way to pass through the world unsullied by its attitudes. God-realization is available to all the pure of heart; it is not limited to those in the Judaeo-Christian enclave.

Religion and Generic Spirituality

There is a distinction between what people usually understand by religion and generic spirituality. Religion is concerned with creeds, codes, and cultic practices, that is, what is approved, said, and done in one's particular religious tradition. The fact that all the world's religions have such characteristics is their common denominator, or what I would call their least common denominator. On the other hand, generic spirituality refers to what is common to them on a superior level, to what is best, noblest, and rarest — to their highest common quality. What I mean is that there is a mystical element at the core of all the great religions: in Buddhism, Hinduism, Islam, Judaism, and Christianity. All have produced outstanding spiritual guides and teachers, men and women who have experienced the divine in a transforming way. This is something that the early zealous missionaries to the Far East failed to grasp in their eagerness to make converts. Many of these benighted heathens had passed beyond the goal of trying to rid themselves of the more obvious moral impediments to spiritual growth. They had advanced to a state where subtle spiritual truths are communicated to the soul, and a few had entered, finally, into the unitive way, where the continual awareness of God is unbroken even amid the need for individuals to occupy themselves with the many obligations imposed on them by their state of life.

What is common to the contemplatives and mystics of all the religions is the sense of awe they experience when they come in contact with the divine presence within them at the center of the soul. One approaches that inner chamber with a good measure of fear and trembling, but also with a sense of boundless love and joy. This poignant bittersweet experience is typical when one is on the threshold of an authentic mystical experience of the ecstatic type. Later, after one has had time to reflect on what has happened, there comes the realization that, beyond sorrow and the uncertainties of embodied existence, the sunny side of our clouded spirit always basks in the divine presence.

Coming down from the mountain, one will almost certainly have to clothe oneself in the garments of one's chosen religion. It can hardly be avoided. Jesus himself could not avoid it completely. But whether ascending or descending, one should not mistake the particular for the generic, the symbol for the symbolized. This would be to fall into the error of the misplaced absolute, and it has been the source of much religious hatred and intolerance, the kind a certain type of religious zealot, who knows nothing about the interior life or contemplative practice, is responsible for. Christians have condemned to the gallows those who, though sincere and basically good people, whether Catholic of Protestant, held views at variance with the views held by those who had the power to kill them — and promptly did so. Thus perished Hus, Becket, Bruno, More, Campion, Cranmer, and Tyndale, to mention but a few. Such attitudes, which in the past were responsible for torture and persecution, are less common today, unless you happen to live in Iran, the Sudan, Yugoslavia, Northern Ireland, or Chinese-occupied Tibet. What is distressing is that people who seem to be essentially sane and decent in the ordinary conduct of their lives can cultivate what are best described as those "sacred hatreds" which pit one people against another on the basis of religion, race, gender, or ethnic origin. Religion, which ought to be the foundation for world peace and understanding, is so often politicized and used to fuel national hatreds.

Fingers Pointing to the Sacred

If Jesus comes to us as the Torah or Word of God clothed in human flesh, *Sacramentum Dei,* Holy Scripture, too, clothes the Absolute in the sacramental garb of words. It provides a storyline that is meant to be evocative rather than literally historical. "Evocative," I think, is an apt word. Most religious scriptures are closer to poetry than workaday prose. Speaking to the deep self, they seek to elicit from it an assent to truths that are already secretly known but can only with difficulty be brought to explicit, surface consciousness. Frederick Franck has called a recent book of his *Fingers Pointing to the Sacred*,[13] a title reminiscent of the Buddhist saying that the scriptures are like "fingers pointing to the moon." They are useful, suggestive, and they do point the way. But one does not stop with them. Used as a launchpad, they do make a fine point of departure. They should not be treated as a port of arrival. They should not be absolutized, for rigid literalism is a subtle and most dangerous form of idolatry. Historically it has led to a great deal of enmity, suffering, and injustice.

The Gospels are primarily spiritual documents, with a background in history, that teach us how to live and love. What Seyyed Hossein Nasr, the distinguished Islamic scholar, has to say when speaking about the Quran is worth repeating and keeping in mind when reading the Bible and especially the Gospels:

> But the Quran, and with it Islam, is singularly indifferent to the merely historical significance of this sacred history. The Quran is not a book of history and is even less concerned with history than is the Bible. The sacred history recounted in the Quran is in reality the epic of the life of the soul. The forces of good and evil mentioned in its pages are to be found within ourselves.[14]

As long as we are an embodied species, we will continue to need external signs and symbols to help concentrate the mind and suggest deeper spiritual truths. Liturgy is the almost universal means used by religion to assist in this task. For some, love of neighbor may be liturgy enough in that it embodies when acted out an implicit creed and a moral code. This does not suffice for the vast majority of people. We require liturgies in the form of civic ceremonies, parades, processions, graduation exercises, marriage rites, flag saluting. The same is true in what pertains to divine worship. When people go to church, synagogue, or mosque, they want something to happen, something to be done. Sermon and song are not enough. Even when clerical plumage, vestments, and statues are discouraged, the most austere denominations will insist on a candle or two and bowed heads at the proper times, not to mention the rites of baptism and communion. Even so, Christians for centuries have run the risk of identifying spirituality with religion, with churchgoing,

---

13. Junction City, Ore.: Beacon Point Press, 1994.
14. *Islamic Spirituality: Foundations* (New York: Crossroad, 1991), 7.

surplice, hymns, and incense. Martin Luther King once told a friend that "religion begins when you leave the church," not specifying whether he meant to spell "church" with a small "c" or a capital.

In one of his talks during his visit to the United States, when he proved to be the star speaker at the First Parliament of the World's Religions in 1893, the astute and urbane Swami Vivekananda made the startling statement that "it is good to be born in a church, but bad to die there."[15] Yet the Swami remained a Hindu to his dying day. He died in India at the early age of thirty-nine in 1902, appropriately on the Fourth of July, America's Independence Day. He had great admiration for the democratic spirit he found in the United States with its relative freedom from rigid class distinctions. By not dying in a church, he did not mean that one should become an apostate and abandon the religion one was born into. He meant that one should not remain forever a child and fail to grow up into a mature appreciation of what all the religions of the world are pointing to, namely, their unity at a deeper level. This is what I call, paraphrasing William James, "The Unity of Contemplative Experience."

The religious spirit flowers in many forms. The constellation of the world's religions constitutes an organism of beliefs and practices for which the mystical spirit is the common thread sustaining them all. It unites them according to what is least contingent, relative, and culture-bound. Mystics and contemplatives the world over have similar experiences. That is one reason why the authentic contemplative is the person least apt to become an exclusivist or yield to the kind of intolerance that in days past justified torture and the execution of dissenters.

Since contemplative experience is pretty much the same everywhere, bound as it is to the human psychological and emotional constitution, it is not surprising that when Buddhist and Hindu monks get together with their Christian counterparts, all find that in some areas they have more in common with one another than with the more popular expressions of their own respective religions. The outward expressions of popular religions vary greatly. So much so, that persons born and brought up in one religious culture can feel very uncomfortable when they are exposed to the traditional religious practices of another. This is where talk of relativism is justified. But one has to penetrate beyond appearances. At the generic level, Buddhists, Hindus, Jews, Christians, and Moslems meet. They are like radii originating at the circumference of a circle and

---

15. *What Religion Is* (New York: Julian Press, 1962), 7.

converging at a point representing the center of the circle. At that point all relativism disappears in the unity of contemplative experience.

The ideal human being is said to be someone who is expert in at least one field, yet with broad interests and wide horizons. The specialist is also a generalist. The same is true in the spiritual life. It is important to belong to and participate in some kind of religious community, in other words to "practice one's religion." That is being a specialist. Beyond that lies the need to be open to and appreciate the worth of religions other than one's own. No one has a monopoly on the Holy Spirit. God is at work everywhere, wherever the living image of God is to be found. The Almighty does not love some and leave others out. We are all divine offspring, beloved children of God, God's kin. Jesus put it in a few well chosen words. Who is his mother and who are his brothers? Not just a Jew or a Christian, but his kinfolk are "those who hear the word of God and do it" (Matt. 12:48; Luke 8:21). He said he has many sheep who are not of the (Jewish or Christian) fold, and that in the kingdom of God and in his Father's house there are many different dwelling places (John 10:16; 14:2). The kingdom is not a drab monotone but a coat of many colors, not a monolith but a many-splendored gemlike thing with myriad facets, all reflecting the immense fecundity of God.

•

It sometimes happens that the words or title of a popular song can be given a religious significance and used as a mantra. Some fifty years ago, there was a popular song which included the words, "The very thought of you. . . . I see your face in every flower, your eyes in stars above." Applied to the contemplative's vision of God, a similar thought is expressed in the *Svetasvatara Upanishad,* which forms the endpiece of this book. St. Paul saw Christ in the members of the early Christian community, and Jesus himself identified with the least of men and women. So when the Hindu sage, writing over a thousand years ago, declares that "the Lord of shining light" is present "in the depths of our heart" and that "All heads are Your Head, all faces Your Face," for "You are the woman and You are the man, You are the youth and the maiden, too," he is speaking for the contemplatives of all ages who see God everywhere. In the Christian idiom this means recognizing that the least member of the human race has been created in the image of God and is to be valued the way Jesus valued each one, that is, as an extension of himself.

THE LORD OF SHINING LIGHT
From the *Svetasvatara Upanishad*

I know You, Ancient One, the Lord of shining light,
Who dwells beyond all darkness and the night;
By knowing You alone can a man cross over death,
There is no other path for him to take.

All heads are Your Head, all faces Your Face,
You dwell in the cave of the heart and all hidden places.
Through the whole universe, You have extended Yourself.
You are Shiva, the auspicious, the ever-present Lord.

With hands and feet everywhere, eyes and ears
Everywhere, heads and mouths everywhere,
You have filled up every corner of space.
Smaller than the smallest and larger than largest.

Present are You in the depths of our heart.
When free of desires and unshaken by sorrow, we
Seek for You only. Then, by Your grace, Your
Form and Your glory stand clearly before us.

You are the woman and You are the man,
You are the youth and the maiden, too;
The old one tottering there with his cane
Is You, who are born here again and again.

You are the bird of dark-blue hue and the parrot green
With bright red eyes; You the thunder-cloud's black sheen,
You are the seasons and the seas. Beginningless and
Endless, You are the One from whom all worlds are born.

Can men ever roll up space like a skin?
Then, unless they have known You without and within,
How can they cross over sorrow and death?
O You, whose light needs no other light.

To You, Lord, I come in my longing for freedom;
To You, Lord, for refuge, with reverence, I come!

— *Translation by Swami Yogeshananda*

p.37
All the way to Heaven is Heaven too.
Catherine of Siena

173   it is good to be born in a church, but bad
to die there.

174-5